HAIL SOPHIA
The HOLY SPIRIT Of WISDOM

Jim McGilbrith

Professor of his love for Sophia.
Department of Religious Philosophy

Providing the Truth in Literary Criticism and Analysis
Of the Wisdom books and Literature of the Bible

For the Jim McG...
Forest School of Philosophy

No portion of this book may be reproduced in any form without permission, except as permitted by US copyright law. For permission contact the author at JimMcGilbrith.com.

Publisher's Cataloging-In-Publication Data
Names: McGalbraith, Jim, author.
Title: Hail Sophia : the Holy Spirit of wisdom / Jim McGalbraith.
Description: Lodi, WI : Forest School of Philosophy, 2023. | Includes bibliographical references.
Identifiers: ISBN 978-1-949085-66-2 (paperback) | ISBN 978-1-949085-67-9 (ebook)
Subjects: LCSH: Wisdom literature--Criticism, interpretation, etc. | Wisdom--Biblical teaching. | Bible--Study and teaching. | Femininity of God. | Women and religion. | BISAC: RELIGION / Biblical Commentary / Old Testament / Poetry & Wisdom Literature. | RELIGION / Biblical Studies / General.
Classification: LCC BS1455 .M33 2023 (print) | LCC BS1455 (ebook) | DDC 223/.0609--dc23.

LCCN: 2023902773

© 2023 Jim McGilbrith
All Rights Reserved

Cover design by Jim McGilbrith
Forest School of Philosophy, LLC
JimMcGilbrith.com

Dedicated to my dad,

a wise and wonderful father who taught me

about God and prayer.

Table of Contents

Preface:
    Why Begin with a Prayer   vi
    The Hail Sophia Prayer   vii

Introduction:
    Solving the Mystery of Sophia   viii

Ch. 1:   Who Is Sophia?   1

Ch. 2:   An Introduction to the Wisdom Books of the Old Testament   16

Ch. 3:   Solomon Seeks and Finds Sophia So Beautiful, He Vows to Marry Her   22

Ch. 4:   The Marriage of Lover and Beloved in Christian Mysticism   40

Ch. 5   Pythagoras Was the First Lover of Sophia, the First Philosopher   56

Ch. 6:   Enlightened Yogis of India Confront Alexander: "God Abhors War"   66

Ch. 7:   How Septuagint Met the Upanishads in Alexandria, Egypt   79

Ch. 8:   The Prophet's Rebellion and the Great Transformation   87

Ch. 9:   Sophia's Instruction Manual on How to Find Her   94

Ch. 10:   Sophia Delights God and Plays with the Sons of Man   104

Ch. 11:   The Best Way to Find Sophia Is by Loving Her   113

Ch. 12:   Where Is This Kingdom of God We Are to Seek and Find?   117

Ch. 13:	Did the "Kingdom of God" Come from the Hindu Upanishads?	125
Ch. 14:	Emperor Constantine Rejects Sophia and Institutionalizes Imperial Roman Law and Conquests	133
Ch. 15:	Jesus and the Evangelists Affirm Sophia Is the Holy Spirit and the Bride	150
Ch. 16:	St. Basil the Great Saves and Defines the Holy Spirit, Like Sophia, but Male	175
Ch. 17:	Jesus' Mother Mary Becomes Our Spiritual Mother	181
Ch. 18:	Meditating on Sophia	187
Epilogue:	Sophia Makes Us an Offer We Can't Refuse	195
Endnotes:		197
Bibliography and Brief Review of Sources:		203
Author Biography:		217

Preface:

Why Begin with a Prayer?

"What is the best way to introduce the reader to Sophia, the Holy Spirit of Wisdom?" I wondered. I thought back on how I learned about God through prayer. When I was a child, my Dad taught me to pray to God as Our Father. He said that God is like my God Father: God created me, He loves me, wants me to be with Him in heaven, and He can hear every prayer I whisper. By describing God as a Person, I had an image of God I could address, communicate with, talk to. I had faith that when I prayed to God as Father, there was a Being of love and caring who listened. It is through this faith and prayer that I created the mental space in which I could communicate with God and in which Sophia, the Holy Spirit, responds.

As Hagia Sophia is a divine Person, the Holy Spirit of God, it seems appropriate to introduce Her through prayer. She is described in the image of our divine Mother and Lover in human terms, and She is gloriously beautiful and easy to think about, to contemplate, or meditate on. The "Hail Sophia" prayer is a compilation of scriptural passages and poetry taken from the Wisdom books of the Bible. As with the "Hail Mary," we address Sophia directly. The prayer also has similarities to litanies honoring the Wisdom Mother of the East and Mother Mary in the West. I say the prayer daily before meditating, generally twice a day when the sun is rising and setting.

The Hail Sophia Prayer

Hail Sophia, the Holy Spirit of Wisdom and Perception,
>	The omniscient, ever presence of God!

You are my Mother, the Giver of Life,
>	Who loves me, cares for me, shelters and guides me.

You are my most intimate Lover, my Companion, my Bride.
>	Come to me, dance with me, hold me ever close to your heart.

You are the Breath, the Energy, the Power of God,
>	The manifestation of God's bounty and Being in the universe.

You are the Eternal Light, the Source of Life and Grace.
>	The wondrous all-pervading Glory of the Almighty.

You are Holy, ever pure Love, Joy, and Peace,
>	The Image of God's Goodness, so attractive and inviting.

Please teach me to live in your Holy Wisdom,
>	To be a friend to God and recognize the Self in others.

Oh, Sophia, you are more splendid than the sun;
>	You outshine the constellations.

Compared to sunlight, you take first place,
>	For daylight must yield to night,

But over you, darkness can never triumph.

Oh Loving Sophia,
>	Show me the Kingdom of God,

That all is the Body of Christ,
>	That I may recognize you within others,

And learn how to treat them as I would be treated.
>	Lead me away from darkness and ever towards your splendor
>	and Light,

That I might die into your loving embrace.

>					Amen/Aum

Introduction:

Solving the Mystery of Sophia

I thought I'd begin by telling the story of how I got involved in this fascinating and rewarding project researching Hagia Sophia, Holy Wisdom, in our Bibles. My dad and I have been associating with each ever since I can remember, and like most father-son relationships, we have had our ups and downs. He was and is a traditional Catholic, a "Do what you are told" disciplinarian, and one humble enough to know the Pope and Bishops knew best on all matters of faith and morality. I suspect youthful rebellion was devised by evolution to propel the young adult out of the home and into the world to think and act independently, but there was an extended period during which we did not talk much, especially about religion.

After a few decades into adulthood, I'm following my religious path, and he's still doing his, except the Catholic church has changed. Perhaps it is hard to tell for those who didn't know it from before, but it is much more open: women are involved, and the church is more tolerant of diversity, but most importantly his Catholic Church began to emphasize God's love for us rather than sin and suffering and behaving ourselves, which for the Irish like me is somehow difficult to do. God as Love was good for Dad. When he retired and was able to spend more time with his family, he opened up and communicated his love, especially to his children and extended family. You might say he became a more loving father rather than a disciplinarian. This was a turning point in our relationship.

Now I know from my reading of Eastern mystical literature that Eastern religious philosophy had a big impact on Christianity. So I decided it would be interesting to have a dialog with my dad about religion in the context of his his belief system. I knew from previous reading there was valid information there we could explore toether as we both loved God.

Impressed by the name, I asked my dad what he thought of the book of Holy Wisdom. As he said it was one of his favorite books in the Bible, I agreed to read it.

So there I was one night sitting in my chair reading the book of Holy Wisdom and I read that Holy Wisdom is the Holy Spirit. (Pause for effect.)

Well I didn't know that, and the next step is even more "shocking." Holy Wisdom is the English translation of Hagia Sophia, Sophia, for short. So what the Bible is saying is that Hagia Sophia (Holy Wisdom) is the Holy Spirit. Did you know that? Sophia is the Holy Spirit of Wisdom and Perception, or Holy Spirit of God, for short.

Let me repeat that so everyone understands the jump we are making. My Bible says that the Greek Hagia Sophia, the Sophia philosophers love, is "Holy Wisdom" in our Bibles, the Holy Spirit of God, who eventually becomes the Third Person of the Christian Trinity, and She Enlightens us.

I Never Heard Sophia Was the Holy Spirit

Reading Sophia was the Holy Spirit surprised me not only

intellectually but emotionally. I was raised Catholic and I listened to Bible readings at Mass, served as an altar boy, went through years of parochial education and high school religion classes, and even took some advanced theology class work at Notre Dame but never heard that Holy Wisdom is the Holy Spirit. What is going on? I decided to research the subject in depth.

This project became a quest to solve what I call "the Sophia mystery." Sophia is very much in our Bible, as the divine Holy Spirit of God, nonetheless, and Christians are generally unaware of who She is or what Her mystical and sacramental roles are in the Judeo-Christian tradition. And yes, Enlightenment is very much a part of the Bible. "The Word is the True Light who Enlightens all human-kind."

The Mystery of the Mary Magdalene and Hagia Sophia Conspiracies

Was there some sort of religious conspiracy to keep Sophia out of the Bible similar to the conspiracy to hide Mary Magdalene's real relationship with Jesus as portrayed in *The Da Vinci Code*? We will never know if Jesus and Mary were intimate, or had a daughter, or if there was a conspiracy to hide such a "fact." We do know that there was a conspiracy against Sophia being the Holy Spirit. We will delve into the matter quite seriously later in the book.

Introductory Matters: The Gender of God

As technicalities such as capitalization and gender are often the cause of misunderstanding, let me tackle these literary issues up front.

When we say that Sophia is the Holy Spirit of God, the first response we expect to hear is, "But She is female and the Holy Spirit is male." That interpretation was a Stoic imperial Roman invention. In

Hebrew, spirit (*ruah*) is feminine. Spirit is also feminine in Aramaic. In Greek, spirit (*pneuma*) is neuter, but *Pneuma Sophia*, the Holy Spirit of Wisdom, would certainly be feminine. Thus, if Jesus was talking about the Holy Spirit formally at a temple, informally with the people, or in philosophical circles, He would have referred to the Holy Spirit as divinely feminine.

But when you think about it, what does gender have to do with God? Are we making God in our image, anthropomorphizing God? If the Holy Spirit is some sort of invisible presence without a body, why do we assign Him or Her a gender?

God made human-kind and the animals down through the evolutionary cycle as either male or female. A person is defined in part by their bodies, especially if it determines how we relate to each other as adults and as children. God as Father and God as Mother are two different images of God existing in cultures throughout the world. They represent slightly different spiritual energies. The image of God as "Father" or "King" or "Lord" would emphasize God's authority. The image of God as Mother would accentuate God's love and caring nature. These images of God allows us to think of God as a "Person," a Being like us rather than some abstract thing like the laws of physics ordering of the universe or "nothingness." The big difference between a person and a thing is that a person can love and be loved, can care about another person. It is because God is a Person, three divine Persons according the Catholic Catechism, that we can have a relationship with Them, we can communicate with Them, we can love Them.

But a friend of mine objected. "God cannot be a person because He is transcendent, beyond human. God is exponentially different from a human being. Therefore you can't call God a person." "But

God is a person," I argued. "That is how God is experienced, as a person, but much, much bigger. If God is not a person, how could God love us? If God were not a person, how could I love God?" We finally decided that God is at least a person, but so much more: God is a "Person" with the "p" capitalized. Similarly, I am a being; God is a "Being;" Sophia is God "Being."

Capitalization

The problem with capitalization in this book comes up primarily because we will be arguing for a divine Sophia who is "the Holy Spirit of Wisdom, the ascendant of the Holy Spirit of Christianity, and thus worthy of having her name capitalized out of respect ("R-E-S-P-E-C-T," think Aretha Franklin) for Her divinity just as we capitalize "He," "Him," and "His" for Jesus and God the Father. I would note when I referred to God as three persons, I capitalized "Them" to indicate all three are divine. The point is, we capitalize words that refer to God to emphasize they are special. God is special, the Giver of Life and Grace, who exists as One Consciousness watching over us all, and turning all things towards good, and not to be forgotten, relating to us as we interface with God individually. This is somewhat amazing that God, who is as bigger than the galaxy, would care about us, but that is a part of the wonder and mystery.

An "avatar" has become both the name of a (pretty good) movie and the name for a personality we take on in playing video games. There is a historical link between the Hindu Trinity and Christian Trinity. An Avatar is an incarnation of the Second Person of the Hindu Trinity, who takes flesh and walks amongst us. Avatars, like Jesus, are always born miraculously to "ever pure," virgin women. The Avatar is the "Word of

God" in Hinduism, maintaining and ordering the universe, and moving all things towards good. The Greeks then Romans took much of the Hindu Trinity to create the Christian version.

So just to be fair, how would Christian parents feel if their kids played with "christs" on their video games shooting and killing each other? So I will capitalize "Avatar" not only out of respect for Hinduism but also out of respect for Jesus Christ, who most Hindus consider an Avatar anyway.

Similarly, there are also two kinds of enlightenment: one spiritual and the other intellectual and historical. I will capitalize spiritual Enlightenment throughout this book, as most English books now capitalize Samadhi, and even Gnosis. It is important that we understand that Enlightenment – "full" and "intimate" knowledge of God – is our inheritance as Jew or Christian.

I will also capitalize identities of what God is. For example St. John writes, "God is Light." Since he is talking about the Eternal Light, which is also divine, it makes sense to capitalize "Light." The same with "God is Love," "God is Spirit," and "God is One." Being "One" is one of God's most important divine qualities.

Bad Western Translations of Jesus' Eastern Religious Concepts

I would also like to address the translation of scripture. There are many translations of the Bible, each trying to be as accurate as possible, according to their political and spiritual ideologies. Then there is the effort to copyright God's word, which I won't get into now. Translating scripture, or interpreting scripture according to your tradition, is a literary craft. It is often interesting to compare passages in different Bibles just to get the nuances. Remember that the Old Testament Bible is a translation of ancient texts collected and selected from different cultural traditions throughout the Mideast, rewritten with Biblical characters, then translated into Greek, then Latin, and finally English. So there is a great deal of opportunity to embellish and enhance the stories.

The problem with Western translations of the Bible is that much of the time they didn't and don't understand what Jesus meant. This is because they try to use the Old Testament monotheistic vocabulary in which God is the creator and perfect, while mankind and the world are created and imperfect. Jesus spoke with an Eastern, non-dualistic vocabulary much of the time. In this system, God is not separate from the universe, but the universe is God Being. "To Be" is a verb. It is also built into the name of God as Yahweh, which means "I Am." In the Eastern system, we are all connected to God as sentient "members" of God's infinite body, the Mystical Body of Christ. We are all a part of God's being. God knows everything that goes on in our minds. Note how the separation of God and human beings inherent in dualistic Monotheism disappears.

Perhaps the "Greatest Commandment" is the best example of this error in Western translations of scripture, as one would assume the "Greatest Commandment" ranks high in defining Christian morality. The first part of the Greatest Commandment is "Love God with your entire heart, mind, and soul." Then, importantly, Jesus says, "The second part is the same as the first: Love your neighbor as your Self." In Hinduism (and Buddhism), the Self is God inside us as Christ Consciousness. The Self inside us also becomes critical in understanding Christ's Mystical Body. We are all members of Christ's mystical body such that "whatever you do to the least of your brothers you do to Me," (Matthew 25) because Jesus Christ is the Christ Consciousness, the Self latent and in everyone.

Isn't it interesting that it can make such a big difference in understanding something as basic and important as the Greatest Commandment by just capitalizing the "s" in "Self?" At the Forest School of Philosophy we do capitalize Self and will comment on differences in translations throughout the book.

Chapter One: *An Overview*

Who Is Sophia?

I expect from the start, few will even know who I am addressing. *"Who is this Sophia you want us to hail?"* For starters, Sophia is an important, transformational character in our Bibles. "Hagia Sophia," Sophia, for short, is translated "Holy Wisdom" in most English Bibles, or sometimes simply "Wisdom" or even just "wisdom." Those who read or were taught the Bible will recognize Her, especially in Proverbs where Sophia introduces the Eucharistic, delights God, and plays with the Sons of Man. She was so popular in Proverbs that She received a follow-up Bible book, the book of Holy Wisdom, featuring Her as the divine, "the Breath of God," the Holy Spirit of Wisdom and Perception. This is a delightful book which contains an in-depth description of who Sophia is and what Her functions are as the Holy Spirit. Having a wonderful Person like Sophia as the Holy Spirit rather than a stodgy "Holy Ghost" makes a big difference in our concept of God.

With Sophia and the Wisdom books of the Bible, we get back to the Judeo-Christian tradition that believed in seeking and finding God, experiencing God intimately, having real Communion with God, and becoming Enlightened. And in order to do this, the ancient Jews and Philosophers meditated on "the Goodness of God." In the book of Holy Wisdom, Sophia is described as "the Goodness of God." In the Old Testament of the Canonical Bible, which was approved at the Council of

Nicaea, we read:

> Happy are they who meditate on Sophia.
>
> Ecclesiasticus 14:20

Did you know that the ancient Jews who wrote the Wisdom books of the Bible meditated? That may be a surprise in and of its self. But an even bigger question pertains to the object of their meditation. Who is this "Hagia Sophia," and what is she doing in our Bible?

Sophia Impacted Our Definition of Who God Is

Just to emphasize how important the character Sophia is in Judeo-Christian tradition, look at the impact She had on our theology and Christology. In the period just decades before Jesus was born, Sophia was described as all the following:

- The Holy Spirit of Wisdom and Perception
- A divine (female) Being of God
- An omniscient (all knowing), omnipotent (all powerful), and omnipresent (all observing) Being
- "The Glory of God," "the Breath of God, "the Power of God"
- "The Word of God"
- "The Giver of Life," our divine Mother
- "The Bride," the divine Being of Light and Love in whom we have intimate Communion (Gnosis/Enlightenment) with God
- "The Eternal Light" who Enlightens all human-kind
- "Ever Pure" and "Holy"
- "The Goodness of God" philosophers meditated on

All these great words of deep meaning describe God as a wondrous Being, do they not? I want to emphasize a couple things from this list we might overlook.

God is a Person

We talked about this in the introduction, but for those who skipped it, let me state it again because it is important. God is experienced as a Person. It is because God is a Person that God can love us, and we can love God. If God were a thing rather than a Person, there would be no caring, no possibility of communication and love. But God is a Person, like Jesus, but also like Sophia. What is special about Sophia is that She is a delightful Person, very attractive and loving. God knows everything we feel and think, sees even the sparrow fall from the tree. That is God's omniscience. Because He knows what is on our minds, we can communicate and even experience God through prayer, meditation, and loving devotion. The Creed says that the Holy Spirit should be "adored and glorified." These are joyful acts of celebrating Sophia as a Person and our relationship with Her.

Note how by recognizing Sophia as the Holy Spirit, God becomes mystically available to us again as a real Person, a Being with real character. She is easy to like and love, unlike the Holy Ghost, who doesn't seem like he has any personality. I find Sophia to be quite attractive and easy to love. She is also active and involved in our lives, giving us shelter, guidance, grace, and Enlightenment. We can communicate with God through prayer; even have intimate Communion with God as Holy Spirit, as Sophia. We can not only believe that God exists, but know God exists through experience. That encourages belief and faith better than anything. In scripture we find the Holy Spirit to be not only a very attractive Being, but someone who loves us and wants us to know Her intimately and be happy with Her investment in us, the gift of Life.

For those seeking a more mystical Christianity, how mystical is that? Through Sophia inspired Christianity we get a relationship with God based on prayer, meditation on a beautiful devine Being, intimate Knowledge of God, Enlightenment, Eternal Life, and Communion with God in the Mystical Body of Christ. Sophia inspires us to seek and find God and love God with all our hearts, minds, and souls.

Enlightenment is Our Inheritance as Christians

With Sophia comes Enlightenment. I have heard some people say that the enlightenment in the Bible is different from that of Eastern religions. This is not true. The Wisdom books of the Old Testament were published in Greek in Alexandria Egypt during the hay-day of philosophy. Pythagoras' followers believed in Enlightenment, karma, the soul, reincarnation, and that Pythagoras was an Enlightened master (like Jesus). Although philosophy certainly diversified later, we find Eastern mysticism and spirituality handed down from Pythagoras to the Platonists to the Neo-Platonists. It was the Neo-Platonist Plotinus who wrote *Towards the One* and inspired St. Augustine to meditate on the "Goodness of God" to experience God. We read about Plato inventing the soul, but certainly you would need a soul to go from incarnation to incarnation and that came from India through Pythagoras as did many of the definitions of God attributed to Sophia.

A note of caution About "Enlightenment:" There are degrees of Enlightenment, and revelations of God are said to be infinite. In this book, which is based in the vocabulary of Wisdom Christianity, I am talking about Enlightenment as a Baptism in the Holy Spirit (Sophia).

Baptisms are, of course, a beginning, not an end. We do not claim the Enlightenment of the Buddha or that of Jesus, or even that of a prophet. At the Forest School, we define "Wisdom Enlightenment" to be a Baptism, a beginning, a realization of a relationship with a Being of God we didn't know was there. Much of this book will be devoted to telling how wonderful Communion with Sophia is. And don't worry, the Wisdom books tell us how and where to find Her. Proverbs especially is like a manual of how to have Communion in Sophia.

Beautiful Poetry Makes the Study of Sophia Easy

We will be defining who Sophia is by first reading the Wisdom books of the Old Testament, then the New Testament to the final passage of Revelations. Generally, I think people regard Bible study to be a chore, especially the lineages and the history of who slew who. However, the Wisdom books of the Bible are entirely different. They are generally written in poetic verse, filled with wonderful metaphors and imagery. Often, the beauty and symbolic substance lie in the underlying theme of romantic love – of seeking the beloved Sophia. Solomon seeks Sophia in his youth and finds Her so gloriously beautiful he falls in love with Her and vows to marry Her. Thematically, their marriage as Lover and Beloved is portrayed in magnificent love poetry in the Song of Songs. All this glorious flattery and love language makes reading about Sophia "easy." Some passages of the Wisdom Literature, especially the Song of Songs, compare well even with *Romeo and Juliet* as an expression of romantic love, but Songs has a much happier ending. As spiritual literature, the Wisdom Literature of the Septuagint-based Christian Bible contains the most extensive and attractive description of God as Holy Spirit available. Solomon, the assumed identity of the author of several of the Wisdom books, was an inspired poet.

In the case of the Wisdom Literature, the media is the message. That is, the language of the Wisdom books of the Bible is designed to change your programming, encourage a jump in our understanding of ourselves, our neighbors, the universe, and our relationship to God in order to increase our spiritual awareness of God as Spirit.

The History of Sophia

In order to understand who Sophia is, you have to know where She came from and how She got into our Judeo-Christian Bibles. A quick glance at history finds Sophia was famous throughout the Mediterranean long before Jesus was born, or the Wisdom books of the Bible were written. Pythagoras was the first lover of Sophia in the West, the first philosopher. ("Philos" is Greek for "to love," plus "Sophy" equals "philosophy.") This gives the word philosophy new meaning. Were philosophers religious? Did philosophers love Hagia Sophia to the extent She was divine? I would point out Solomon, the wisest man on earth and presumed contributor to several Wisdom books, was certainly a lover of Sophia. We have his word for it in the Bible. And there was also the important theologian Philo, who popularized Sophia in Alexandria Egypt – it seems he was also a lover of Sophia. So we know that in Alexandria, philosophers who happened to be Jewish loved Hagia Sophia and regarded Her as divine, and I expect many philosophers around the Mediterranean loved Sophia, but that is kept from us as religious philosophy was defined as Pagan. Yet, philosophy as it was practiced in Alexandria, complete with its sacramental rites and sects, was the basis of Christian practice as well as its Theology.

Where did Pythagoras find out about Sophia? – In India of all places. In his youth, Pythagoras traveled the world seeking truth. He visited India and the temple caves of Ellora and Elphanta. These temples are now an important tourist site in India where the East's influence on Western religions is better recognized. Now we begin to see the link to the East and how meditation and Enlightenment and words with deep, mystical meaning got into our Bibles.

Sophia's Role in the "Great Transformation"

In examining Western history, we realize Sophia played a "transformational" role in our spiritual and religious history. Here I am referring to Dr. Karen Armstrong's classic *The Great Transformation*. In her book, Dr. Armstrong argues the emergence of religion comes from a spiritual repulsion to the suffering and cruelty of war. We agree with Dr. Armstrong that in the Jewish tradition this occurred with the Prophet books. We agree that it is in these books that the prophets turned against their religious rulers and railed against them for their injustice. The major Prophet Isaiah tells the religious high priests of the day that God is repulsed by their bloody, stinking sacrifices and holocausts of dead animals. Through Isaiah, God actually tells the temple priests to "go away" from Him, He doesn't want to see them anymore. There are some great insults in Isaiah, but we will save them for later as we discuss the scene in more detail, giving the reader something to look forward to.

The reader will remember from the Creed that the Holy Spirit speaks through the prophets. Not incidentally, Isaiah is the first book in my Bible I have come across where we are directed to "seek and find."

What God Wants and Doesn't Want

Well, if God doesn't want sacrifices and holocausts of rams and sheep, what does He want? Hosea eloquently says what God wants and doesn't want.

> God wants compassion, not sacrifices.
>
> God wants intimate knowledge of God, not holocausts.
>
> Hosea 6:6

Dr. Karen Armstrong defines the type of knowledge God wants as follows.

> He did not mean theological knowledge: the word *Daath* comes from the Hebrew verb *yada*: to know, which has sexual connotations. Thus J says that Adam knew his wife, Eve.
>
> A History of God (1)

The "knowledge" that God wants us to have of God is like the same kind of knowledge Adam had of Eve, a man has of a woman, a woman of a man, and the ever virgin Mary had of no man (purportedly). This is intimate knowledge indeed. This sort of intimacy is useful in explaining why sexual union is used in the Bible as a great metaphor for Communion with God in the Song of Songs. Alternatively, St. Paul refers to the kind of knowledge we have of God as "full knowledge of God." But adding the intimacy with the sexual metaphor is poetry. God wanting Enlightenment or Communion with human beings is encouraging. If God wants Enlightenment, who can argue with that? Understand that Communion comes from the Latin "Comm-" means "of" and "-union" means union. When Jesus was alive, there was, a union with God in Communion, God enters our consciousness and makes it bigger. Did you know that God wants Holy Communion with us?

Sacrifices and holocausts, what God doesn't want, have commonly become metaphors for wars and genocides. "Sacrifices" refers to the suffering of soldiers and civilians killed or maimed in war. This term is actually used in military planning to describe possible loss of lives. We thank dead soldiers for their sacrifice. We also sacrifice the solders to the homeland or the higher cause we are fighting for. Generally, counties war because they cannot pay their debts and need to acquire more capital and charge higher rents. "In war, people have to make sacrifices." Holocausts have, of course, come to mean genocidal mass murders of one group by another. We agree with Hosea, God does not want wars and holocausts, and we make the case that "God abhors war."

In contrast God wants us to be compassionate towards and seek Enlightenment through love and devotion. Through communion with God, we realize the value of ourselves and each person to God. We consider the choice between "compassion" and "Enlightenment" versus "sacrifices" and "holocausts" to be one of the most important ideological dialectics that drive human history.

The History of Sophia Is Epic in Scope

After Pythagoras, we follow Sophia through history and discover how She got into our Bibles. This story features many of history's most important characters, the "Greats" at pivotal times in our religious and political history. Our cast of characters includes Alexander the Great, Emperor and Saint Constantine the Great, and St. Basil the Great, all of whom played key roles in the Church's and Sophia's history. We will see Brahman yogis confront Alexander the Great on his imperial conquest into India: "God abhors war." We even engage the name of Cleopatra as the Wisdom books of the Bible were written in Ptolemaic Egypt, at the Great City of Alexandria during her rule there. We will observe how the Ptolemaic Dynasty commissioned the seventy-two Jewish scholars to write the Old Testament in Greek for the Jewish room of the Great Library of Alexandria and the population of educated, Greek-speaking Jews living in Egypt. And we must not forget Jesus, who was very much in love with Sophia, for She is the answer to the question, "To whom was Jesus the groom?"

The Wisdom Literature of the Bible is literary and theological genius, the history you will read in this book is epic, the religious and spiritual issues we wrestle with are essential to our understanding of who we are and what our relationship with God is. Does God even exist? How do we know? Who or what is God? What kind of relationship can we have with a God or how do we find a God who is invisible?

My Personal Search for Sophia

I think it is interesting to relate my personal history to this whole story of Sophia in the Bible. As Roman Catholic kids in parochial school, we were well indoctrinated on the importance of the Trinity, the three divine persons in one God. We did the sign of the cross before saying prayers, after praying, and when scoring a touchdown to thank God for the play, or to give credit to God for my good play, or something like that. Although some still cross themselves today, I'm talking the mid to late 1950s. At that time the Holy Spirit was called the "Holy Ghost." Now for me, as the youngster that I was, ghosts were kind of scary. I really didn't know much about ghosts – I hadn't really seen one. All I knew was that ghosts were dead people flying around making weird sounds and acting scary.

In many ways, the Catholic understanding of the Trinity during the 1950s was conveyed through the Irish cultural idiom. All Catholics in my neighborhood knew that St. Patrick taught the Irish about the Trinity using the shamrock: "The Trinity is like a shamrock. There is one plant, but three independent leaves, just like there is One God but three divine Persons." Thus, the term "Holy Ghost" retains a flavor of Irish folklore for me. You can almost hear an old Irishman tell his grandson about the shamrock and the Trinity with an Irish brogue: "And, my lad, the third person of the Trinity is the Hooly Ghooste."

Back in the days of my youth, Walt Disney made a movie called *Darby O'Gill and the Little People.* The movie was certainly great Irish storytelling, but given my childish imagination and innocence, some of the action scared the dickens out of me. Oh, there were ghosts all right – I saw plenty of them in the movie. There was the screech of the banshee as the poor lost soul flew about, lost in the netherworld. And then there was the dreary coach of death driven through the dismal, dark, rainy night by none other than Mr. Death himself. And the carriage is coming down for poor Darby O'Gill and lands in his front yard. Well, in the end he is saved, but I decided it might be best if I waited to make the acquaintance with this "Holy Ghost" person. But then nuns and priests who taught me did not really talk very much about this "Ghost of God" anyway, which was fine with me. Changing the name of the Holy Ghost to the Holy Spirit was a big deal to me.

I don't remember any prayers to the Holy Spirit. It didn't seem peculiar to me then, but does now. Doesn't it seem peculiar that there are no prayers to the Holy Spirit, who is supposed to give us grace and council, inspire us and pick us up when we are down? But even though "He," the Holy Spirit, is to be "adored and glorified as the Father and Son" in the Nicene Creed, I neither adored nor glorified the Holy Spirit. It was not part of the curriculum. I prayed more to my Guardian

Angel and St. Michael the Archangel than I did to the Holy Spirit. It is interesting in retrospect, I said the most prayers to the Blessed Virgin Mary, Mother of God.

My College Years During the Vietnam War

When I started college, my country, the United States, was fighting its war in Vietnam. The events were shocking, the daily count of body bags, bombing peasant villages, torture and murder in the night, and B-52s eradicating forests and blowing up people. Then there was the famous image of the napalm-burned Vietnamese girl running naked from her village. The institutional church supported the fight against "Godless Communism" that threatened to pick off our Democratic governments and turn them into Communist regimes. Nations would fall like dominoes.

Catholic colleges, including both St. Norbert's (important as it was the site of the G.B. Packers training camps back in those days) and Notre Dame, supported ROTC programs as military service was "our religious duty." But to me, war is not Christian at all. People are proPagandized to hate others of different cultures, races, religions, and people considered to be the enemy deemed insignificant. Hate turns to murder, murder to torture, mass murder, mass burial graves, and rape. Imperial wars are simply institutionalized murder for financial gain and vain glory. That we still engage in forever wars, and spend trillions to threaten and bully others, is a black mark on our nation, the human race, and the Judeo-Christianity tradition.

I was of draft age, and Uncle Sam wanted me to kill the Viet Kong for him, so this was an existential moral question radically impacting my direction in life. And so it was that the war in Vietnam divided American society, the church, the faculty at Notre Dame, and me from traditional Christian political society.

God Might Be Dead in the West, but He Can Be Found in the East

At about the same time frame in collective memory, *Time* magazine famously headlined in bold print the shocking question: "Is God Dead?" Because of the sharp irony of the meme, the question caught on and spread. Although the Time article addressed the commercial and materialistic culture in America, the question in my mind was the agnostic's question: If you can't see or hear or sense God in any way, is He really relevant to our lives? You might blame youth, you might blame commercialism, but attendance at daily mass at Notre Dame was down, and the priests let us know they were disappointed.

But then later, the Beatles and an ex-Harvard professor and LSD pioneer named Richard Alpert (Ram Dass) went to India and found God. God might be "dead" here in the States, but word was you could find Him alive and well in India. Based on what we read, lots of people found God in India. Their testimony was sincere. They found God, all humankind was one family, and it was wonderful. So began the generational migration movement East, searching for a real God who could actually be experienced and was relevant to our lives.

So this is a full circle. I started out in the West but could get no peace because there was no intimate experience of God, no Enlightenment, no Sophia. I went East and found the divine feminine in the Wisdom Mother and Shakti, the Holy Spirit of the Hindus. Thus coming back into contact with Christianity through my Dad, I recognized Sophia when I discovered Her right there in my Jerusalem Bible he had given me for Christmas four decades earlier.

Sophia and the Coming Renaissance of Christianity

We hear that Western society is now in the post-Christian Era, and this is something that is good. We hear the priests are lechers, the Papal See corrupt, and the churches of Europe are empty. I have read that we are exiles from true Christianity, and that *Christianity must Change or Die*. (2) I humbly offer Sophia, the Holy Spirit of God, as the possible "change" that could not only write the Church but lead to a Renaissance in Christianity. After a minor admission of a Roman Emperor's mistake in interpreting scripture during the institutionalization of the Church (which everyone already recognizes), the Church gets to reclaim a Holy Spirit with soul and personality.

Christianity is not going away any time soon because of the contribution Jesus made to our understanding of ourselves and God's love for us. Jesus belongs to the world; He frees all humanity and gives us the status of the children of God. Jesus is honored as an Avatar in India, a Prophet in Islam, and Jesus' lifetime, death, and Resurrection will inspire spiritually oriented people through time. His words will not go away because they are Dharmic, the Truth, if interpreted properly. By interpreting scripture correctly, we find Sophia and our salvation.

The problems of Christianity are not of Jesus making but of the modern scribes and Pharisees and the emperors and prelates who institutionalized Christianity. What is presented to us in traditional Christianity is not the Christianity Jesus intended. Christianity was intentionally broken by Constantine at Nicaea by rejecting Sophia as the Holy Spirit and legitimizing imperial law, a societal structure including slavery and a legacy of war as a necessary institution of the state. True Christianity, Jesus Christianity, is Wisdom Christianity, and Sophia is the Holy Spirit of Wisdom, who is One with the Christ in essence and mission.

The Wisdom Books of the Bible Describe the Mystical Method to Know God

The Wisdom books of the Bible document the mystical method for seeking and finding God in the West and is the same as finding God in the East. Philosophers, the Jewish authors of the Septuagint Bible and early Christians, including St. Augustine, all meditated on the "Goodness of God." In the book of Holy Wisdom, Sophia is defined as "the Goodness of God." And Ben Sirach, the author of Ecclesiasticus, confirms his use of the same meditation on Sophia, "Happy are they who meditate on Sophia" (Ecclesiasticus 14:20). Focusing the mind in meditation is not an easy process. I know scores of people who meditated for a while on mantras made of abstract sounds or simply on breathing. But meditation on Sophia is much easier because She is so gloriously beautiful and willing to reveal Herself to those who seek and love Her. And Sophia wants Enlightenment, to have intimate Communion with us also. So let's end this first chapter with Her invitation to a romance and adventure of a life-time.

> The Spirit and the Bride say, "Come."
> Let everyone who listens answer, "Come."
> Then let all who are thirsty, come:
> All who want it may have
> The water of Eternal Life, and have it for free.
>
> > Revelations 22:17

Chapter Two: *The Wisdom Books*

An Introduction to the Wisdom Books of the Old Testament

Our research into Sophia begins in the Canonical Bible, specifically in the Wisdom books of the Old Testament. The Wisdom books of the Old Testament listed in my Bible are Job, Psalms, Proverbs, Ecclesiastes, the Song of Songs, The book of Holy Wisdom, and Ecclesiasticus (the book of Sirach). These books were written late in the Greek period, after the Pentateuch and most of the historical books. Although many of the psalms and proverbs date from antiquity and thus are quite old, the Wisdom books are collections of documents discovered, selected, edited, transcribed, and published late in the Greek period, much of it probably during the last century, before Jesus was born.

Scholars call this period of Jewish literature the "Greek Period" because Greek philosophy dominated educated circles throughout the Western world and the authors of the Wisdom books spoke and wrote in Greek. The spiritual system of philosophy overlapped Eastern religions, not only relating to reincarnation and Enlightenment but also as to how they practiced prayer and meditation.

I read somewhere that during Cleopatra's lifetime, which ended only about thirty years before Jesus was born, India was Egypt's largest trade partner. This seemed strange as Alexandria is on the Mediterranean

Sea and thus much closer to Italy and Greece than India. I was able to document that trade with India was certainly Egypt's most profitable.

> Egypt's profitable luxury trade was with India; lustrous silks, spices, ivory, and elephants traveled across the Red Sea and along caravan routes.
>
> Cleopatra, a Life (3)

The commercial trade between Egypt and India during this period is documented by other scholars.

> To the south, in the Indian Ocean, up to 120 substantial Greek ships a year plied between the Red Sea ports and India, exploiting the monsoon, while Arab ships traded from port to port along the north-west coast of India. Since then ships with a carrying capacity of up to 500 tons sailed with the monsoon winds across to the Indian ports. In winter the winds reversed and the Greek ships returned laden with products of the East.
>
> Times Atlas of World History (4)

In Alexandria with its cosmopolitan library, trade in commerce encouraged trade in ideas and ideals. It was at the great Library of Alexandria that Buddhist monks and Hindu yogis mixed with rabbinical students and philosophers and debated religious and moral theology. The contributions of Greek philosophical theology and Eastern mysticism are evident in the Wisdom books of the Bible.

The Poetic Style of the Wisdom Books of the Bible

The language of the Wisdom books of the Old Testament is much different from the Pentateuch and other historical books, which rely on declarative sentences to describe Jewish history, or what was forbidden and punishable in the legal books. The difference in style is initially recognized as most of the Old Testament Wisdom Literature is broken down by line and verse as poetry. One might expect Psalms to be broken down in this fashion as songs are often based on poetic verse. My Bible even includes the instrumentation for Psalms. Similarly, the Song of Songs is broken down by line and verse as romantic love poetry, as sensuous as anything Shakespeare wrote. I have seen Songs published in artfully designed poetry books, but I have never heard it sung. Many of us remember the song "Turn! Turn! Turn!" (written by Pete Seger, a hit single sung by the Byrds in the 1960s). The words of the song were taken from Ecclesiastes and matched with a catchy melody. Much, but not all, of Ecclesiastes, is written in poetic form in my Bible. Although the subject matter of Job would not seem to lend itself to poetry, it is translated line and verse, again, in my copy. The books of Proverbs, Holy Wisdom, and Ecclesiasticus (also called the book of Sirach) are also written in the poetic "Wisdom style."

This poetic Wisdom style – vocabulary, imagery, and metaphors – is also used widely in the New Testament, but especially in St. John's Gospel, his Epistles, and Revelations, as well as St. Paul's Epistle to the Ephesians.

My Youthful Wonder at the Prologue to St. John's Gospel

It is important to see how the Wisdom language and meaning of the Old Testament translates into the New, that it is used by Jesus. A prime example is the prologue to the Gospel of St. John, which was also originally written in Greek. I remember as a youngster first reading the prologue to St. Johns Gospel in a new missal with a larger page size allowed it to be broken down by line and verse like poetry, and the words and ideas seemed to have a hidden meaning that I could not understand at the time. What was this "Word" they kept talking about? What beginning? The prologue had a mystery to it that fascinated me:

> In the beginning was the Word.
>
> The Word was with God.
>
> And the Word was God.
>
> Through him all things came to be.
>
> Not one thing had its being but through Him.
>
> All that came to be had Life in Him.
>
> And that Life was the Light of men.
>
> A Light that shines in the dark,
>
> A Light that darkness could not overpower.
>
> The Word was the True Light,
>
> Who Enlightens all humankind.
>
> John 1: 1-5, 9

Note the power of declarative sentences when used poetically. We read a series of very short declarative sentences that define the Word to start: "In the Beginning was the Word. The Word was with God. The Word was God." Not only is the language different than what I was used to, but the words are filled with possibilities. "The Word was the True Light, Who Enlightens all humankind."

As we proceed in our study of Sophia, we find all these theological concepts, "the Word" and "the True Light," and the Person who "Enlightens all humankind," were all attributed to Sophia during Jesus' lifetime. We will go over this passage line by line later in the book.

The Purpose of the Wisdom Books of the Bible

The writers of the Wisdom books of the Bible wrote with intent. Their intention was to teach. In my Bible, the heading of the first chapter of Proverbs is "The purpose of this book:"

> For learning what wisdom and discipline are,
> For understanding words of deep meaning,
> For acquiring an enlightened attitude of mind
> Virtue, justice, and fair dealing;
> For teaching sound judgment to the ignorant,
> And Knowledge and sense to the young;
> For perceiving the meaning of proverbs and obscure saying,
> The sayings of sages and their riddles.
> Let the wise listen and he will learn yet more,
> And the man of discernment will acquire the art of guidance.
> The fear of Yahweh is the beginning of knowledge,
> Fools spurn wisdom and discipline.
>
> Proverbs 1:1-7

Proverbs, the primer in the Wisdom books series, is for learning, understanding, and acquiring a different way of thinking about life, God, and the universe in which we live. In a later chapter focused on Proverbs, we will examine this passage line by line, but note the intent. I have seen philosophy described as an educational system, and we see this clearly in this passage. The intent of the passage is to change the way we think so we understand who we are and what our relationship to God is.

The Wisdom Language of Metaphor and Parable

Jesus said, "The kingdom of God is like a mustard seed…" As a direct statement, this makes little sense. *How is the kingdom of God like a mustard seed?* we ask ourselves. Jesus responds, "They both start small and grow to a large size." *Huh? Where does the kingdom of God grow into a tree?* Taken literally, parables often don't make sense. There has to be another level of meaning, a different way of thinking about the kingdom of God. Often a parable is a play on words where a word or phrase (like the Kingdom of God) will take on a mystical meaning most people don't understand. The idea is to draw the reader into a word puzzle that makes them make a jump in reasoning to solve it. I would not be the first to compare Jesus' wisdom parables to Zen koans, which also ask similar seemingly impossible questions to answer. For example: "What is the sound of one hand clapping?" This seems to me to be similar to Jesus asking if we have "ears that hear."

Chapter Three: *The Book of Holy Wisdom*

Solomon Seeks and Finds Sophia So Beautiful, He Vows to Marry Her

The book of Holy Wisdom is written in two parts. The second half of Wisdom is an interpretation of Jewish history as "wise" in the historical sense. Hagia Sophia, generally translated Holy Wisdom, is featured in the prologue, which includes chapters one through eight. I would expect Sophia was quite popular in Her role in Proverbs, which was published earlier, so She won a starring role in the book of Holy Wisdom. I expect Wisdom was published in part as people wanted to hear more about Her. Wisdom was a publishing hit, and it made it into the Septuagint Bible. In the book of Holy Wisdom, Sophia appears center stage as the spiritual protagonist of the book.

According to the editors of my Jerusalem Bible, (5) the book of Holy Wisdom was written not by Solomon, the heir of King David as the narrator portrays himself, but by a learned "Hellenized Jew" in Alexandria, Egypt, during the late Greek Period.

Dating the Book of Holy Wisdom

The editors of my Bible date Wisdom "towards the middle of the first century BC." However, looking at their methods of dating, there is much uncertainty, and it may have been written even later, closer to Jesus' lifetime. The best source of information on the dating of the book of Holy Wisdom is through the writings of Philo, an enthusiast of Sophia, who was an important scholar and teacher in Alexandria, Egypt, around the same time Jesus lived. I would note that the name Philo is a play on "philosopher" where "philos" means "to love," indicating he was "a lover." He was also enthusiastic about Sophia and the book of Holy Wisdom, which he wrote about extensively, so I expect he was also a lover of Sophia. As Jesus was expert in the Wisdom language, and spoke in Parables using words of deep meaning, I fully expect Jesus read the book of Holy Wisdom as well as the other Wisdom books of the Bible.

Seek and You Will Find

Solomon begins the book of Holy Wisdom with the "seek and find" theme. I found this initially surprising, but then realized this is perfectly consistent with the Wisdom Literature. Note that in Wisdom, the object of our seeking is well defined. We are to seek "the Lord" God.

> Let honesty prompt your thinking about the Lord.
> Seek Him in simplicity of heart;
> Since He is to be found by those
> Who do not put Him to the test.
> He shows Himself to those who do not distrust Him.
> But selfish intentions divorce one from God;
>
> Wisdom 1:1-3

So first, we are to seek and find our Lord God. God shows Himself/Herself if we are pure/simple of heart. This is reflected later in the New

Testament with Jesus observing the Beatitude, "Blessed are the pure of heart, for they shall see God."

Sophia Is Identified as the Holy Spirit

The first chapter of the book of Holy Wisdom continues and directly addresses Sophia as the Holy Spirit:

> No, Sophia will never make Her way into a crafty soul,
> Nor stay in a body that is in debt to sin;
> The Holy Spirit of Instruction shuns deceit ....
> The Spirit of the Lord, indeed, fills the whole world,
> And that which holds all things together
> Knows every word that is said.
>
> Wisdom 1:4-5

Sophia is identified as the "Holy Spirit of Instruction" through parallel sentence structure. The Sophia "who never makes Her way into a crafty soul" is the same as the Holy Spirit who "shuns deceit." In the Jewish poetry style of the times, parallel sentence structure indicates an alternate description of the same thing, including Sophia as the "Holy Spirit of Instruction." Also, note that Sophia "fills up the whole world" and "knows every word that is said" indicating She is omnipresent and omniscient (all knowing).

But as there is no "is" identity statement, and it is a big jump to identify Hagia Sophia as the Holy Spirit, let's examine a parallel passage from Isaiah where the Prophet describes the Holy Spirit:

> A shoot springs from the stock of Jesse,
>
> A scion thrusts from his roots:
>
> On him the Spirit of the Lord rests,
>
> A Holy Spirit of Wisdom and Perception,
>
> A Holy Spirit of Counsel and Power,
>
> A Holy Spirit of Knowledge of and the fear of the Lord.
>
> Isaiah 11, 1-2

Here is our "is" statement, and later we will get others. "The Spirit of the Lord" God is identified as "The Holy Spirit of Wisdom and Perception," which is one of Sophia's best titles.

Why Did God Create the Universe?

One of philosophy's biggest questions is, "Why did God create us? Why did God go to all the trouble to make the universe?"

We have heard the suggestion that God was lonely, and as Love itself, He needed somebody to love. So He created rocks and trees and birds and bees and human beings to love, and eat each other (irony intended), thus incorporating the problem the Buddha had with life: "Life is suffering." *Did God make us to love us or torment us, or love the ones who love Him and punish those that don't? Is God selfish? Is God using us for His entertainment?*

The book of Wisdom offers a much better answer for why God made us.

> To Be – for this God created all things.
>
> Wisdom 1:14

This is so simple and logical, but the impact of this realization is immense. Absolute Consciousness wants to Be, to express His/Her creativity and experience Life. The universe is God Being. We are all a part of God Being.

The translation of "Yahweh," one of God's names in the Old Testament, is "I Am who Am," which can be shortened to "I Am." God Being is the cause of the universe, the energy of the universe, and the purpose of the universe. The "I" of the "I Am" is Christ Consciousness, the Big Buddha, Shiva, the One God. You will recognize them when you meet Him. "Am" is the activity of God being the universe, which becomes the bounty of Christ, the Word of God, the energy and power of God, or Sophia, the Holy Spirit of Wisdom and Perception. The mystery is that Sophia and the Christ Consciousness are One.

The concept of the universe as "God Being" is present in ancient Hinduism. In the famous statuary of Shiva as "Nataraja," Shiva dances with the universe, his hair flying and legs moving as fast as time within a giant wheel of time and space. This portrayal of God is visible throughout India, including at the temple caves that Pythagoras visited at Ellora and Elphanta.

Sophia Becomes Divine

As we proceed to the seventh chapter of Wisdom, Solomon seeks Hagia Sophia in his youth and finally finds Her. He describes Her as a Person, a divine Being who is glorious, beautiful, and pure love beyond measure. Solomon pours out his heart, expressing his love of Sophia, his dedication to Her, and in the end he vows to marry Her.

As this is some of the best religious poetry ever written, here is the passage in its entirety without comment:

Sophia is quicker to move than any motion;
>She is so pure,

She pervades and permeates all things.

She is the Breath of,
>And the Power of God,

The Pure emanation of the Glory of the Almighty;
>Hence nothing impure can find a way into Her;

She is the reflection of the Eternal Light,
>Untarnished mirror of God's active power,
>Image of His goodness.

Although alone,
>She can do all;

Herself unchanging,
>She makes all things new.

In each generation she passes into holy souls,
>She makes them friends of God and prophets;

For God loves only the man
>Who loves Sophia.

She is indeed more splendid than the sun,
>She outshines all the constellations;

Compared with light,
>She takes first place,

For light must yield to night,
>But over Sophia evil can never triumph.

She deploys her strength
>From one end of the earth to the other,

Ordering all things for good.

Wisdom 7:24-8:1

So now the reader knows where I got most of my language for the prayer at the beginning of this book.

Have you ever wondered what God is like, who God is? Well, the Holy Spirit is God and this is the best description of God as Spirit I have seen in the Bible or anywhere in religious literature, in my opinion.

In a passage preceding the one above, Solomon provides a litany of Sophia's qualities:

> Sophia is...
> Intelligent, holy,
> Unique, manifold, subtle,
> Active, incisive, unsullied,
> Lucid, invulnerable,
> Benevolent, sharp,
> Irresistible, beneficent, loving to man,
> Steadfast, dependable, unperturbed,
> Almighty, all-surveying,
> Penetrating all intelligence,
> Pure, and most subtle spirits;
>
> Wisdom 7:22-24

These descriptive words are listed in litany format to be read, pondered and reflected on before moving to the next. Although some of these words seem to tell us more about what is going on in Solomon's mind than in Sophia's, Sophia inspires these feelings and concepts. The last lines show that Sophia is omnipotent (almighty), omnipresent (all-surveying), and omniscient (penetrating all intelligence or consciousness), and thus divine.

Breaking Down Sophia's Description Line by Line

Let's take this passage apart line by line, starting with verse 25.

> **Verse 25, Line 1**
> *She is the Breath, the Power of God,*

This passage is proof that Sophia is the Holy Spirit with an identity "is" statement. The "Holy Spirit" simply is "the Breath of God." That is one of the most basic and ancient definitions of the Holy Spirit. The Holy Spirit has always been the "the Breath of God" that gives us Life. In Genesis, God breathes Life into Adam. In the Nicene Creed, the Holy Spirit is "the Giver of Life." I am capitalizing "Life" here as "man does not live by bread alone," and this "Life" is spiritual, the union of individual consciousness with the senses.

The nature of the Holy Spirit as "breath" is also built into our language. In Latin, both "respiration" and "inspiration" are derived from the Latin root word *spiritus* meaning "spirit." The Greek word for spirit, *pneuma*, is translated by English scholars as "energetic air," sometimes as "a great wind," but *pneuma* is better translated as "breath" or even directly as "spirit" in ancient times.

Solomon next says that Sophia is the "Power of God." Again, this was the definition the Jewish philosophers had for the Holy Spirit at the time this was written in Alexandria, Egypt. Here is Philo, the Jewish theologian and contemporary of Jesus, from *A History of God*:

> Philo (made) an important distinction between God's essence (*ousia*), which is entirely incomprehensible, and His activities in the world, which he called His "powers" (*dynameis*) or "energies."
>
> A History of God (6)

According to this model, God has two aspects. First there is a transcendent Godhead, who is beyond our understanding, and then there is the "power" or "energy" of God, who is active in the World as God's Spirit. And it is no accident that in Wisdom, Sophia is "the power" of God. On a macroscopic level, She is as big as the universe and orders all things for good. Yet on the personal level, we can communicate with Her as a mother or Lover.

> **Verse 25, line 2**
>
> *(Hagia Sophia is) a Pure Emanation of the Glory of the Almighty.*

Every time I think about this line, I end up smiling and thinking, "God, what a beauty She is!" She is indeed glorious.

This line also describes how She comes out of God: She "emanates" from Him like light energy coming from the sun and filling space. To have Sophia emanate from God, She must be a part or aspect inherent in God that is already there. The Spirit of God is certainly a part of God, perhaps God's essence.

When I think about the "glory" of God, I always end up thinking about sunlight, perhaps how good it feels in the morning on a clear day, and Solomon does th same. But according to Solomon, Sophia is more glorious than even the sun itself:

> **Chapter 7, Verses 29-30**
>
> *She is indeed more splendid than the sun,*
> *She outshines all the constellations;*
> *Compared with sunlight, she takes first place,*

For daylight must yield to night,

But over Wisdom *evil can never triumph.*

Before Jesus was born, Sophia played the role of the Eternal Light who Enlightens all humankind. This is "the Light that shines in the darkness," in the prologue to St. John's Gospel. In his Epistles, St. John says, "God is Light." As the Holy Spirit of Wisdom and Perception, Sophia is that glorious Eternal Light.

Chapter 8, Verse 1

She deploys her strength
From one end of the earth to the other,
Ordering all things for good.

If Holy Wisdom is God's "Power" and "Energy" active in the world, what does She do with it? What is Her function? Sophia "orders all things for good." Turning all things towards good has always been the function of "the Word of God." In this passage, written just before Jesus was born, Sophia is the "Word of God," and the energy and power of God, who orders all things for good.

During difficult times, especially in times of political struggle or war, which seem to be our constant predicament, this passage has given me some reason for hope. We hope there is some learning there, but it is sure slow. As a species we are quite given to fighting politically to get our way and winning. We like fighting for a cause, for truth and justice or whatever ideology we are attached to. It makes us feel important. "Turning all things to good" must be a long-term project for Sophia.

Chapter 7, Verse 26

She is the Reflection of the Eternal Light,

Untarnished mirror of God's Active Power,

Once again the writer associates the Eternal Light to Sophia. No surprise. However, the "reflection" and "mirror" wording of the passage is perplexing. First it says Sophia is the Eternal Light. Then She is the "reflection" of the Eternal Light. If She is the "energy and power of God" in one line, why does She become the "mirror" of that power in a later line?

The reference to reflection had me stumped for some time until I thought of a metaphor from the Hindus that says the reflection of the sun in the full moon is much easier and more attractive to look at than the sun itself, which is too bright. In this metaphor, God is the sun, which we cannot see, and Sophia is the reflected light of the sun, which is so dear to look upon. This metaphor is one of the ways the Hindus work within the monotheistic framework and still makes Shakti, the Holy Spirit of the East, divine and attractive.

The "mirror" is what the reflection of God bounces off of and usually refers to the "mind" or consciousness itself. The idea in Hinduism is to keep the mirror of the mind clean and clear.

The use of language in these lines is based on metaphors allowing for a transcendent God whose reflection in the world is Sophia. However, we find the translation of this language confusing.

Third line, Verse 26

(Sophia is) the Image of God's Goodness.

This is another important line. Philosophers, including the writers of the Septuagint Old Testament, early Christians, including St. Augustine and probably Jesus and the mystical St. Paul, meditated on "the Goodness of God" to experience God, to be Enlightened. Who is the Goodness of God? This verse tells us. It is Sophia. They meditated on Sophia. Sirach confirms their happy practice in Ecclesiasticus: "Happy are they who meditate on Sophia."

Sophia Is Omniscient, Omnipotent, and Omnipresent

According to the Greeks, Buddhism and Hinduism, and the Roman Catholic Church from its inception, God is defined to be omniscient (all-knowing), omnipresent (present everywhere), and omnipotent (all powerful). Solomon, the narrator in the book, describes Sophia as having each of these qualities of God:

> Hagia Sophia is Omnipotent:
>> Sophia is "Almighty."   – Wisdom 7:23
>> Sophia "can do all."   – Wisdom 7:27
>> Sophia "deploys her strength from one end of the earth to the other, ordering all things for good."
>>> – Wisdom 8:1
>
> Holy Sophia is Omni-present:
>> Sophia "pervades and permeates all things."
>>> – Wisdom 7:24
>> Sophia is "All-surveying."   – Wisdom 7:23
>
> Sophia is Omniscient:
>> Wisdom "Penetrates all intelligence" [our minds].
>>> – Wisdom 7:23

Verse 23, line 4

Penetrating all intelligence,..."

This an interesting way to say Sophia knows what we are thinking and feeling, what is on our minds. This is how She knows we are praying to Her, how She knows we love Her – because She shares our minds. But we usually do not find this kind of language to explain omniscience. Where does it come from? The Upanishads, ancient Hindu Scripture, explain where this concept of omniscience comes from:

The self existent Lord pierced [penetrated] the senses
To turn outward.
Thus we look to the world without
And do not see the Self within.

Katha Upanishad (7)

This is quite the image – God looking through our eyes and hearing through our ears. We think we are what our senses tell us, rather than our inner Christ Consciousness, which turns out to be what Hindus call the Self.

Wisdom – Chapter 7, Verse 24

Sophia is quicker to move than any motion,

This is another example of the overlap between the Upanishads and the language of Wisdom. This verse sounds like a roundabout way of saying Sophia is omnipresent. It makes more sense if you know it comes from the Upanishads.

(The Lord is) ... swifter than thought, swifter than the senses.

Though motionless, He outruns all pursuit.

Isha Upanishad (8)

The idea is that when you are in one place, there is God, and then when you move to another place as fast as you can, God is there, too. Wherever you look, wherever you are, there is Sophia.

Part of our practice will be noting Sophia is always here with us all the time, not as judge, but our Lover who gives us Life (Consciousness), Being, Grace, the waters of Eternal Life, and intimate Knowledge of God, Enlightenment. Her intention is to "turn all things to good" even for us personally.

Verse 24 continues

Sophia is so pure;
She pervades and permeates all things.

Purity is something that I have come to appreciate only lately. Back in the old days, impurity was generally associated with sex and having "impure thoughts." The Virgin Mary, for example, was pure because she was ever virgin. However, the idea of this sort of purity being good became unpopular as who wants to remain a virgin. However, purity actually refers to a quality of mind. It pertains to having selfish desires. We might admit to selfish desires, but do we want that quality in God? Do we want an "impure" God who wants, who manipulates the universe for His pleasure? In contrast, Sophia is Holy and pure, She is not selfish but entirely loving and giving. Her love is Life and grace given to all freely. What we do with it is up to us. It is through Her grace and love that we are given "free choice." As Sophia is pure, Her love is pure. She wants nothing but our betterment.

Solomon's Reaction to Finding Sophia

So the book of Holy Wisdom begins with Solomon seeking Sophia, and in chapter seven he finds Her:

> I prayed, and understanding was given me;
> I entreated, and the Holy Spirit of Wisdom came to me.
> Wisdom 7:7

Solomon's love and prayer are rewarded. He asked, he sought Sophia, he knocked and the door was opened, and the Holy Spirit of Wisdom, Sophia, revealed Herself to him. This is a wonderful passage in Wisdom. It documents Solomon's Communion with Sophia.

Solomon delights in Her company:
> I esteemed Her more than scepters and thrones;
> Compared with Her, I held riches as nothing.
> I reckoned no priceless stone to be Her peer,
> For compared with Her, all gold is a pinch of sand,
> And beside Her silver ranks as mud.
> I loved Her more than health or beauty,
> Preferred Her to daylight,
> Since Her radiance never sleeps.
> In Her company all good things came to me –
> At Her hands riches not to be numbered.

All these I delighted in, since Holy Wisdom brings them.
But as yet I did not know She was their Mother.

Wisdom 7:8-12

When St. Aquinas experienced God, he said all his own writings and words were "like straw." To Solomon gold and precious stones are "like mud" compared to Sophia. I expect they were referring to the same experience. Solomon is very happy with Sophia; She fulfills all his needs and makes him happy.

In the last line of the above passage, Sophia is referred to as the "Mother." Mother here is a reference to the divine Wisdom Mother of India, who is regarded as the source of all good things, just as Sophia is for Solomon.

How Do We Find Sophia?

Solomon's description of his experience of Sophia is meant to motivate us to similarly seek Sophia. In chapter six of the book of Holy Wisdom, Solomon tells us how to find Her:

Sophia is bright, and does not grow dim.
She can readily be seen by those who love Her
And found by those who look for Her.
Quick to anticipate those who desire Her,
She makes Herself known to them.

Wisdom 6:12-14

Here is the mystical secret of knowing Sophia. You look for Her because She is desirable, so attractive, and you find Her by loving Her. As Sophia is so gloriously beautiful, loving Her comes naturally.

Sophia Becomes the Bride

After Solomon describes how wonderful it is to know Sophia the Holy Spirit of Wisdom, Solomon confesses his love for Her and resolves to marry Her:

> She it was I loved and searched for from my youth;
> I fell in love with Her beauty.
> I resolved to have Her as my bride,
>
> *Wisdom 8:2*

She will be with him in good times and bad.

> I therefore determined to take Her to share my life,
> Knowing She would be my counselor in prosperity,
> My comfort in cares and sorrow.
>
> *Wisdom 8:9*

This sounds like a perfect marriage, does it not?

Here, Solomon introduces perhaps the best, most humane and powerful metaphors for Communion with God: the marriage of Lover and Beloved. Jesus later adapts this metaphorical marriage with Sophia. We remember that Jesus claimed He was "groom," but to whom? By reading the Wisdom books we see the metaphor that later explains Jesus' marriage with Sophia as the Holy Spirit, so they become One.

The Best Way to Know God

So the best way to know God fully and intimately is through love and devotion. This should not surprise anyone who has read the Greatest Commandment: "Love God with all your heart, mind, strength, and soul." God is a Person, a Being and loves us and wants Enlightenment, to have union-Communion with us. Most Christians emphasize not being sinful and going to heaven after we die. But love of God provides the underlying motivation for acting as we should. If we love God, why would we do something that would hurt God or our neighbor as we are to love our neighbor as our Self? Whatever we do to our neighbor we do to Jesus Christ as Christ Consciousness. Actions come from the heart. Love God, love neighbor, and things should take care of themselves, wouldn't you think?

Sophia Is God, the Holy Spirit of Wisdom

In the book of Holy Wisdom, written just before Jesus was born, Holy (Hagia) Sophia was divine, fully omniscient, omnipresent, and omnipotent. Sophia was portrayed as "the Word of God," "the Breath of God," "the Power of God," the Glory of God," "the Eternal Light," who Enlightens all humankind, and the Holy Spirit of God, the third Person of what became the Christian Trinity. If nothing else, understanding Sophia's roles in contributing to both the theology of the Holy Spirit and the Christology that later defined Christ is key to understanding the development of the Christian definition of God.

In addition to motivating us to seek and find Sophia, the book of Holy Wisdom tells us how to find Her. The best way of finding Sophia is by loving Her. Through loving devotion we open our hearts to Sophia and make ourselves available to Her. In the Hindu East, they call this devotion to God, *Bhakti*. If you love God with all your heart, mind, and soul you have "Kevala Bhakti," total love for God, and you become God's love or Enlightened. Devotion super-charges prayer, meditation, song, and dance, which are all wonderful, joyous, and "easy" ways of expressing love for God.

Chapter Four: *The Song of Songs*

The Marriage of Lover and Beloved in Christian Mysticism

In the previous chapter on the book of Holy Wisdom, we found Solomon seeking and finding Sophia. He finds Her gloriously beautiful and falls in love with Her and vows to marry Her. In the Song of Songs we explored the theme of marriage as a metaphor for Communion with God. In fact, we get even more intimate as we follow the Bride and Groom as they consummate their marriage in what religious writers and scholars now refer to as "the Bridal Suite of Judeo-Christian Mysticism."

I expect the Song of Songs is probably one of the more widely read books of the Old Testament but less at the pulpit than in a room of one's own. It is love poetry at its best, a delight to read, but with ample metaphorical depth and meaning to last as a classic.

A Very Brief History of the Songs of Songs

The Song of Songs is also attributed to Solomon. Although some of the romantic poetry may be ancient (5th Century BCE, according to the editors of my Jerusalem Bible (9), the actual book was probably drawn from several sources, then combined, edited, and polished, then translated into Greek, or written in Greek, during the late Greek Period in Alexandria, Egypt, by Hellenized Jews writing and translating for the Septuagint Publishing Company and the Hebrew room at the Great Library of Alexandria.

The two protagonists in Songs are identified as "Bride" and "Groom" in my version, making their metaphorical meaning obvious.

The Meaning of The Songs of Songs to the "Youth" Audience

Because of the moral tension between what we regard as "pure" and "Holy" and "sex," we rarely read from the book of Songs during Sunday sermons or in Catechism classes. Rather, we hear it read in youthful weddings when the bride and groom are allowed to pick their own readings from the Bible. The celebratory language fits both their romantic attraction and their love for each other, which is celebrated by the chorus of friends and family.

Songs is a celebration of love and marriage, romance and sexual attraction. The Groom finds his Bride to be very beautiful, and tells her. The language is quite sensuous – full of smell and touch and feelings.

> You ravish my heart
> With a single pearl of your necklace.
> What spells lie in your love,
> How delicious is your love, more delicious than wine!
> How fragrant your perfumes,
> More fragrant than all other spices!
> Your lips, my promised one,
> Distil wild honey,
> Honey and milk are under your tongue;
>
> Songs 4:9-11

"Honey and milk under your tongue?" That is getting intimate. I also enjoy the allusion to "spells," a woman's magical charms, that run deeper than just her physical charms. But we also hear about her breasts and how attractive they are to Him.

> Your two breasts are two fawns,
> Twins of a gazelle,
> That feed among the lilies.
>
> Songs 4:5

Similarly, the Bride finds the groom physically appealing. As a sampling, here are the opening lines of Songs:

> Let him kiss me with the kisses of his mouth
> Your love is more delightful than wine;
> Delicate is the fragrance of your perfume,
> Your name is like oil poured out,
> And that is why the maidens love you.
>
> Songs 1:1-4

And the Bride also finds touching Him to be exquisitely pleasurable.

> His lips are lilies,
> Distilling pure myrrh.
> His hands are golden, rounded,
> Set with jewels of Tarshish.
> His belly a block of ivory
> Covered with sapphires.

> His legs are alabaster columns
> Set in sockets of pure gold.
> His appearance is that of Lebanon,
> Unrivalled as the cedars.
>
> Songs 5:13-15

Although sensuous, with allusions to sexuality, Songs is poetic, romantic, sexy, but never really crass or pornographic. Songs emphasizes the attraction of the Lover and Beloved. Rather, I like to compare Songs to *Romeo and Juliet*.

> What light from yonder window breaks?
> It is the East, and Juliet is the sun.
>
> Romeo and Juliet, II, 2

Ah, feminine beauty once again portrayed as gloriously attractive, like the light of the glorious sun.

I understand that thick anthologies of Shakespeare's at public libraries open naturally to the balcony scene where Romeo pours out his love for Juliet, and Juliet falls for him. We love this sort of romance. What attraction! What love! What poetry!

This romantic and somewhat erotic approach is a literal interpretation of Songs. It does celebrate the romantic love between lovers with breasts and thighs and desire for each other, and the fullness and wonder of their experience of each other. And yes, the young couple getting married in church has a right to celebrate the fullness of their romantic love for each other. The Upanishads explain: "From fullness comes fullness, and fullness remains." Certainly, romantic love and the communion of souls in sex is part of the bounty of Christ, one of the wonderful creative opportunities God gives us. We will discuss hindrances to this persuasion a section or two later.

Marriage as a Metaphor for Communion with God

The Song of Songs is included in the Wisdom books section of my Bible, which hints that something else must be happening on a metaphorical level, which is also why it ends up in the Bible. The concept of the marriage of the Bride and the Bridegroom become well established in the Wisdom books of the Old Testament, and later becomes a part of Jesus' repertoire in the Gospels. How would we know what Jesus was talking about when He claims to be the Bridegroom if we did not know the Bride and Groom in books of the Song of Songs and the book of Holy Wisdom?

The Bride and Groom Are Depicted as Divine

Although playing in the realm of the senses, the Bride and the Groom take on divine roles. In the opening verses, "The King has brought me into his room," the footnotes in my Bible states: "Yahweh is the king of Israel." In the New Testament, Jesus claims the role of Bridegroom, as the Son of God.

The female protagonist of the story, the beloved, becomes the metaphorical Bride. In some passages she seems quite human, loving God as the human Solomon loved Sophia. I can understand a woman loving God as Christ and as Krishna, but you don't have sex with God, do you? But perhaps sex is a metaphor for something greater?

In other passages the Bride becomes the source of grace, "a fountain of Living Water."

> She is a garden enclosed,
>
> My sister, my promised bride;
>
> A garden enclosed,
>
> A sealed fountain....
>
> A fountain that makes the gardens fertile,
>
> A well of Living Water,
>
> Streams flowing down from Lebanon.
>
> Songs 4:12,15

"A well of Living Water..." This is the same "Living Water" that Jesus was referring to when He offered "Living Water" to the woman at the well. This is where Jesus got the metaphor from. We will go over the story of the woman at the well in more detail in a later chapter.

For Mystics, Songs Is About Communion with God

Mystics are even more enthusiastic about Songs than the young couple getting married. For mystics, Songs celebrates our Communion with God as our Eternal, most intimate Lover who knows us inside and out.

So first, let's establish the foundations of the relationship between human beings and God. We can relate to God as a Person. The experience of God is interpersonal – we have Communion with a Being, a Consciousness.

Mutual attraction is another way romantic love and loving God are alike. God is infinitely attractive to us. We are naturally spiritually attracted to God. In the Song of Songs, the Bride and the Groom are drawn to each other physically like magnets. Their passion for each other is obvious. Mystics say that our attraction to God is even stronger.

The mystics say that God is Joy, Love, and Light; God is wonderful. They tell us finding God is the goal of life.

As we are attracted to God, God finds us to be very attractive also, and wants to have Communion with us. God as Sophia invites us with "Come" to Her. We remember from Hosea that God wants Gnosis/Enlightenment. In the East, they say God is waiting for us to acknowledge Him/Her, that if you take one step towards God, God will run to you.

In Songs, God wanting to have communion with us is portrayed in the Groom's, the Christ's invitation to the bride (us) to be with Him:

> Come then, my love.
> My lovely one, come.
>
> Songs 2:10

The invitation is repeated twice, again in verse 13. This "come" invitation is characteristic of Sophia's throughout the Bible. She invites us over and over again to "come" eat Her bread and drink the wine She has prepared. Then at the end of the Bible, "Come and drink the water of Eternal Life for free." We are all invited to the banquet Jesus and Sophia have prepared.

So we have a being of God who is gloriously attractive and inviting, offering us the waters of Eternal Life. How can you turn down an offer like that?

Songs, Sex, Intimacy, and Communion with God

One of the ways that sex is like Communion with God is they are both an intimate way of knowing the other. Dr. Armstrong notes that the kind of knowledge Hosea says that God wants has a sexual connotation. It is the kind of knowledge Adam had of Eve but the Virgin Mary had of no man. (8) This is intimate knowledge indeed. In Enlightenment, we realize God knows everything about us inside and out as everything we feel, think, or remember is a reflected on God's larger Consciousness. We are naked before God, all our thoughts, desires, and fears. God knows everything about us, all our stupid stuff. At the same time, we experience God's gift of Life, which is love energy that is pure, Holy, and unselfish. God wants nothing for His/Her Self, only for us. This contrast of God's purity and our own egocentric natures, always thinking of "me" and "mine," is uncomfortable and humbling. Our sins are revealed and we are naked before God. Although we are humbled, this knowledge that God is a glorious Being who loves, cares for us, and gives us Life unconditionally, is wonderful and should be sought by all. Through intimate knowledge of God we find God is real. We are all connected in one over-seeing Consciousness.

Communion with God Is Pleasurable

Communion with God is also like sex in that they are both extremely pleasurable. Mystics use words like "bliss," "ever new joy," or "Ananda," to describe the joy of God Communion. St. John says God is Love and God is Light, the Hindus say God is Ananda. Even in somewhat prudish India, we hear saints talk about Samadhi as every cell in your body having an orgasm. Others simply talk about the intensity of the Spirit's energetic impact on the human nervous system. The Upanishads say Communion with the Lord of Love exceeds what can be experienced in the mundane world:

> (Knowing God) is the supreme goal of life,
>
> The supreme treasure, the supreme joy.
>
> Those who do not seek this supreme goal
>
> Live on but a fraction of this joy.
>
> The Forest Upanishad (10)

Thus, we have saints in both the East and West, including Solomon, writing wonderful romantic poetry comparing their intimate experience of God with trysts with a lover.

Love Poetry from the Celibate

But do mystics really think like this about God? – Of course. Woman monastic nuns were the first to adopt the idea of saving themselves as virgins to marry Christ in heaven. But what if you don't have to wait until you die? What if you can have Communion with God even in a nunnery? And yes, sometimes it gets romantic. Here is some love poetry about God by a celibate, female saint, St. Catherine of Sienna:

> They kiss sometimes when no one is looking,
>
> The sun and the moon.
>
> Why are they so shy before us?
>
> Haven't we all seen someone make love?
>
> I wept once for three days because He would not touch me.
>
> Was this not a bride's right to know Him?
>
> I have seen what I want in heaven's shop.
>
> Crazed I have become for this.
>
> He was sitting in a window one day, my Lord,
>
> When I walked through the sky's streets.
>
> St. Catherine of Sienna (11)

How many love songs have been written about one lover pining for the comfort and touch of the other? And so St. Catherine pines for her beloved Jesus.

Seeking and Finding the Beloved

We notice in Songs that the seeking then finding is cyclical. In part, this is due to it being several poems linked together, but the general plot seems to be they seek each other, find each other beautiful and attractive, and there is so much talk of love, then the Groom goes off somewhere, apparently, because he has something better to do. The Bride finds she is alone, and starts seeking her Lover again. And it seems St. Catherine lived the same fate, as her Beloved was also absent for days.

This reminds us that our relationship with God is not necessarily linear. Maybe we ignore God for decades, then circumstances and karma, perhaps a death in the family, renews one's interest. Then, if one does have a mystical experience, we find it is initially temporary. And then we are back in the world of commerce, politics, and competition pining for God. But there is always a longing to get back, and we can get partway there anyway by meditating on God's glorious reflection in Sophia.

The Bridal Chamber of Judeo-Christian Mysticism

Because of the confluence of spiritual Communion and the romantic Communion of Lover and Beloved in Songs, we now read in the more recent religious literature of a "Bridal Chamber or Suite of Judeo-Christian Mysticism," in which Lover and Beloved consummate their marriage. This concept comes from this passage:

> ... I found Him whom my heart loves.
> I held Him fast, nor would I let Him go
> Till I had brought Him
> Into my Mother's house,
> Into the room of Her who conceived me.
>
> Songs 3:4

And we will cut from that scene in chapter three to a similar promising scene in chapter five.

> Bridegroom:
>> Open to me, my love,
>> My dove, my perfect one,
>> For my head is covered with dew,
>> My locks with drops of night.
>> I have taken off my tunic.
>> Am I to put it on again?
>
> Bride:
>> My Beloved thrust his hand through the hole in the door;
>> I trembled to the core of my being.
>> Then I rose to open to my Beloved,
>> Myrrh ran off my hands,
>> Pure myrrh off my fingers,
>> Onto the handle of the bolt.
>> I opened to my Beloved ...
>
> Songs 5:2-5

So this mystical love poetry is a delight, and tells us a great deal about our searching for God, our longing for God, and the mystical path.

Is Sex an Appropriate Metaphor for Communion with God?

The problem with comparing sex to Communion with God is we face in many religious circles that sex is impure, and perhaps even dirty. Is animal sex really an appropriate metaphor for Communion with a God who is all pure and Holy? Isn't sex worldly, impure, dirty, and selfish? Isn't God Pure, Holy, and transcendent above all this human fleshy mating stuff?

But Communion with God is really not having sex with God. It is a metaphor pertaining to the mystical exchange of energy and the joy, pleasure, and love we feel in expanded Consciousness. God as Spirit does not have a physical body, and really, our sex organs aren't actually involved. The Communion takes place in consciousness, the mind, not the physical body, and in this state consciousness is expanded. It is not communion with someone with a physical body, but Communion in, with, and through the Holy Spirit. The experience of God, although intimate, is Holy and pure, full of Light and Love and full of life-giving energy. Holy and pure are the opposite of dirty and impure.

Note, it is God as Holy Spirit who is inviting us, not a prostitute. Note that intimate Communion with God is what God wants. We needn't feel guilty about having Communion with God.

The World of the Senses and the World of Spirit

One might have noticed that the young couple in the youthful marriage audience celebrate their passion for each other, but St. Catherine is celibate and eschews such a relationship. The couple is devoted to each other; St. Catherine is devoted to her Jesus. The nuns and monks of both the East and West renounce the world of commerce and the senses to focus on God. They take vows of poverty, chastity, and obedience as they consider riches, the whole mating and marriage scene, "I'm number one," and "I got to be me" to be a distraction from God. They take Jesus literally when He says seek the Kingdom of God first, before anything else. Like Sophia, these vows of Catholic nuns and monks, poverty, chastity, and obedience came from India. In this manner the monastic faithful of both the East and the West yoke the desires of the body so that they can direct the mind to God. That is the theory.

Is the repression of the human desire to possess, to procreate, to win, "to be me," justified? The problem with animal bodies is they want. They want food, they want sex, they want pleasure, they want to possess, and they want to win. Jesus says people who want more and more "live in poverty." This want, this need for more, entangles the heart and keeps us from searching for our Home.

The Yogis teach that if we pursue the world of the senses, if we live like animals, we will end up disappointed, frustrated, and die like an animal. The idea is that if we pursue our natural instincts of seeking sex, gaining possessions, and winning, we will end up being imperialists and conquerors living in a hellish world. The problem is it is our animal desires which we try to satisfy in order to be happy.

In "serious" meditation, there is a process of concentration. The last step before you Commune with God is "pratyahara" or withdrawal of the senses from the body. Some yogis do accomplish this as demonstrated by the yogi who immolated himself before Alexander's army. The followers of this tradition would say that the world is one thing and what is Spiritual is another, that you really do have to transcend the senses and the world in order to be Enlightened. As we noted previously, there are different kinds and degrees of Enlightenment. Perhaps this is who the Enlightenment of the Buddha is like. But we at the Forest School of Philosophy hope to offer an "easier" way.

It is our philosophy that we live in the Kingdom of God full of the bounty of Christ and saturated with God and wonder. We access this kingdom through prayer, meditation, and loving Sophia.

In Hinduism they generally divide a person's lifetime into stages of education for the youth, then career and family for the middle aged in which the adults have certain duties to perform in life, then in retirement for the aged withdrawing from the world and its duties in retirement. Retirement is the time when we can do what we want and spend our lives philosophizing, teaching, and devoting our lives to loving Sophia. That path seems to come naturally for many of us.

I would like to emphasize here that you don't have to be a saint to know God. There is a tradition in most religions that you must live a saintly life in order to have Communion with God. However, that is not the way it works; life and karma are not linear. There are many examples of people not being perfect and experiencing God. In fact, according to many accounts, God seems to come in our most desperate hour. God chooses the time when we are ripe and open, and then there She is. You don't have to be a saint, but most have faith that God exists, love God, and seek to experience God. If you love God with your entire heart, mind, and soul, and your neighbor as your Self, you are practically there.

The Climax of Songs is Perplexing

Back to the story in the fifth chapter of Songs: The Bridegroom is knocking at the door, and she opens to him, but the next line is a surprise.

> But he had turned His back and was gone!
> Songs 5:6

I feel cheated. *Why did He leave? Doesn't he love Her? What a fickle jerk!* I would note that this happens in the fifth chapter and our romantic couple goes on seeking and finding each other for several more chapters. But this is as close as they get to actually knowing each other intimately.

So all that the mystical audience has left is a tail of unrequited love with the Bride can get from her beloved is his hand sticking through a hole in the door in the third chapter. What kind of communion is that?

There are two problems here. Let us solve them separately.

The "door" is a metaphor for our separation from God. We remember Jesus promising, "Knock and the door will be opened." Here, we are surprised as the door does not entirely separate us from God – there is a hole in it. Perhaps prayer is the hole, the secret way of talking to God. But in Enlightenment, where does God come from? She is right there in your own consciousness, and what door? The door seems to have a hole in it. You are never entirely separate from God.

The second problem is, "Why does the Groom turn away in chapter five?"

Frankly, I don't like this ending. If I were writing this as a sacred love poem, I would have the two lovers embrace in prelude to the obvious, and then turn the camera away as in a Bollywood movie. But the editors of my Jerusalem Bible (12) offer an explanation. The bride is playing the metaphorical role of "unfaithful Israel," and the Groom turns away according to the "prophetic formula" of "the withdrawal of Yahweh from unfaithful Israel."

So the Bride in Songs *was unfaithful? I didn't see any of that. Where was She unfaithful? And where is our Communion with God?*

In a sense, this is an ancient Jewish literary technique. They will make you want something and then take it away because you are unfaithful to God, to show how important it is to be faithful to God. But it also shows the tension between the three audiences and the committee of writers. It seems Songs is the combination of several related poems put together by a committee of three. One wanted to celebrate the beauty and bounty of God's creation as manifest by the beauty of the marriage of man and wife. Another wanted to emphasize the possibility of Communion between God, as Groom, and His Bride, and how wonderful it could be. The third writer wanted to make it a metaphor for prophetic rejection of Israel for being unfaithful to God, possibly indicating that the mystic does not deserve Communion with God because he was sinful and only human.

Frankly, I just jettison the third writer and the Bridegroom turning away because that is not how our love affair with God ends. There is Communion with God. I then let the first two: life as the bounty of God, the Energy of God, the Kingdom of God laid out for us to enjoy, and the mystical Spirit available beyond the senses, lay side by side until they both become transcendent.

Chapter Five: *Pythagoras*

Pythagoras Was the First Lover of Sophia, the First Philosopher

In order to understand who Sophia is in our Bibles, we are going to have to go back in history to before the Old Testament was published, back to the ancient Greeks, back to the first philosophers. We remember that in the first chapter summary, I noted that Pythagoras was the first lover of Sophia, the first philosopher ("philos" = to love + Sophy = philosophy). This is the story of how Pythagoras discovered Sophia.

Pythagoras was an intellectual, religious, and spiritual giant in his day, a key figure in the history of Western religion and theology, and yet most in the West regard him primarily as the mathematician who formulated the Pythagorean theorem. However, Pythagoras probably learned the Pythagorean Theorem from the Egyptians or East Indians, who had previously used the formula. Pythagoras taught and wrote about the Pythagorean Theorem in the West to show how the world worked according to certain natural laws, including the laws which could be expressed as mathematical ideas.

However, Pythagoras most important contributions were in the way of Philosophy and Theology. Those in the know call Pythagoras "the Buddha of the West" because of Pythagoras's contribution to Western understanding of God, and because he lived at the same time as the Buddha (563-483 BCE).

Pythagoras Youthful Journey in Search of Truth

Pythagoras's life parallels Jesus' in interesting ways. Pythagoras' birth and great stature were foretold not by an angel of God but by the Delphi Oracle. Pythagoras was born in Syria, not far from the Holy Land. His followers believed Pythagoras was conceived without the benefit of sex. This uncommon means of conception is called "pangenesis," and it is the standard manner in which Hindu Avatars come into the world. Pythagoras's followers believed that Pythagoras was divine, an Enlightened master, a *Sat Guru,* who voluntarily came down from heaven to educate mankind.

Pythagoras's father was a wealthy merchant who traded throughout the navigable world of that time. Similarly, Jesus is closely associated with Joseph of Arimathea, a legendary trader of metals and gems from one end of the Roman Empire to the other. According to legends, Jesus visited both Britain (famous for its lead and tin deposits) and India (long noted for the appreciation of gold, pearls, and light-filled gems) with Joseph of Arimathea.

In his youth, Pythagoras took advantage of his father's connections and traveled the world seeking spiritual truth. Pythagoras visited a number of countries including Egypt, Persia, and India, where he is known to have discussed religion and spirituality with the Brahmin priests:

> While in India, Pythagoras visited the Brahmins. There, worthy priests communicated deep insights to Pythagoras regarding aspects of the mind, the nature of the soul, means of solving the vicissitudes of life, and methods by which man becomes a positive agent in his evolutionary

process. He was allowed to share in profound doctrines taught at Elephanta and Ellora.

Pythagoras: His Life and Teachings (13)

It is interesting that Thomas Stanley's 1678 classic on Pythagoras quoted above is still cited as the best source of information on Pythagoras. It seems there was more interest in Pythagoras specifically, and in all things Greek in general, at our universities in the seventeenth century than now.

What Did Pythagoras Find at the Temple Caves?

The temple caves of Elephanta are located on an island off the western coast of India; the Ellora temple complex is in India. The temple caves and shrines are a well-known and oft-visited UNESCO tourist site primarily because those in the East know Pythagoras visited there. In the West, we prefer not to know that Hindus influenced Pythagoras, or that Pythagoras influenced Christianity, because they were deemed to be "Pagan."

The temple caves are dedicated to the worship of Shiva and Shakti. The many sculptures carved into the cave walls were used to teach people different models or concepts of God through symbolic metaphor. (14)

Temple Images of Shiva

Much of the statuary in the caves represents Shiva in different representations of God. There is the famous sculpture of Shiva as "Nataraja" – Shiva as God dancing the universe, the universe as God Being, His long dreadlocks flying within the rim of time and space. Here, God as Shiva is active in time and space rather than separate from it. There is also a grotto in which the Shiva lingum is displayed. The lingum represents Shiva's phallus, which becomes a metaphor for God's relationship to the universe. The universe is a part of God's body, God's most sensitive part. In these images of God, there is one God, but it isn't Monotheism as we know it. In traditional monotheism, God is the Creator and the universe is created and not only imperfect but "not God." In these depictions of God at Elphanta, the universe is God, it is God dancing, it is God Being. It is the same with the Shiva lingum. Although a part of God remains transcendent, the universe is part of God's body – His most sensitive part. Once you get the image of God being the universe rather than being separate from it, we get an entirely different perspective of who God is and His/Her relationship to us. We find God is not as far away as we thought.

The Marriage of Shiva and Shakti

There is a saying in Hinduism, "Where there is Shiva there is Shakti," and the cave temples are no exception. Who is Shakti? Shakti in Hinduism is described the same way Sophia is described in the book of Holy Wisdom. Shakti is the Holy Spirit of Hinduism. On the macroscopic level, Shakti is the creative "energy" or "power" of God, which manifests as the universe. On a personal level, Shakti is a real Person with whom we can have a personal relationship. In India, Shakti gives us grace and Enlightens those who believe in Her and love Her, just like Sophia in Wisdom.

In the temple caves, there are also several sculptures featuring the marriage of Shiva and Shakti. In one sculptured images celebrating their marriage, we see Shiva and Shakti embracing. In another depiction, the loving couple dances together. These are well-established themes in

Hindu art and literature. The union of Shiva and Shakti is mirrored in the entire pantheon of Hindu Avatars. Shiva is mated to Shakti, Sita to Rama, and Radha to Krishna. Below, Ramakrishna explains what all these marriages and dancing together are all about:

> The heart melting Krishna is actually Pure Consciousness. His captivating consort, Radha, is the primordial energy of Pure Consciousness that projects complex worlds of name and form. What is the meaning of their ecstatic union, depicted by the traditional icon of Radha and Krishna dancing side by side, merged into a single current of Divine Delight? The interpretation is simply this. Pure Consciousness and its own Primordial Power are one Reality, not two. You cannot realize the Absolute without participating in the dance of the relative.
> Ramakrishna, The Great Swan (15)

Note the similarity between Radha, Shakti, and Sophia, as all three are referred to as the "energy" and "power" of God. There is also a parallel between Krishna and Jesus Christ. Both are the second Person of their respective Trinities, and human incarnations of God. Krishna's "Pure Consciousness" Is the equivalent to Jesus' "Christ Consciousness," which we are all connected to, so we are all members of the Mystical Body of Christ.

The Wisdom Mother of India

We can't talk about the divine feminine in Hinduism without discussing the Wisdom Mother of the East. Shakti and the Wisdom

Mother have different names, but they are both closely associated if not inseparable. One of the functions of the Wisdom Mother is to give us "Holy Wisdom," or direct knowledge of God, Enlightenment. The Wisdom Mother is also the giver of Life, even the giver of Eternal Life. She cares and shelters us just like Sophia.

God as Mother appeals to God's loving, caring side and is quite popular in India and is enjoying increasing interest in the West. In late nineteenth century Bengal, Ramakrishna started a religious Renaissance in the belief of God as Mother. In the East as well as New Age Western circles, worship of the Wisdom Mother now vies with Krishna in popularity. The divine feminine is also gaining adherents even in Christian circles. All the notoriety surrounding Mary Magdalene relates to the Christian desire for a woman to be God or to have Communion with God, even physically. Sophia, the Holy Spirit of Wisdom and Perception is already in the Bible and fills the job description perfection.

The Wisdom Mother Appears in the Christian New Testament

Entirely overlooked by most Christians, the Wisdom Mother actually makes an appearance in the Gospels:

> For John the Baptist comes, not eating bread, not drinking wine, and you say, "He is possessed." The Son of Man comes, eating and drinking, and you say, "Look, he is a glutton and a drunkard, a friend of tax collectors and sinners." Yet Sophia (Holy Wisdom) has been proved right by Her children.
>
> Luke 7:33-35

Logic would have it that if Jesus and John are children of Sophia, then Sophia is the Mother of Jesus and John. Now, that certainly sounds like a theological scandal.

But the punch line to this story is even more interesting in Matthew where the same scene is worded a bit differently.

> For John came, neither eating nor drinking, and they say, "He is possessed. The Son of Man came, eating and drinking and they say, "Look, a glutton and a drunkard, a friend of tax collectors and sinners." Yet Sophia has been proved right by Her actions.
>
> Matthew 11:19

Quite surprisingly, Jesus' actions are identified as Sophia's actions. How are either St. John's actions or Jesus' actions the actions of Sophia? Does Sophia act through them, like the Holy Spirit speaks through the prophets? Does She inspire their actions?

The Hindu Trinity Influenced the Development of the Christian Trinity

The cave temples of Elphanta also contain a depiction of the *Trimurti*, the Hindu Trinity. This sculpture portrays God as three persons: Brahma, (the Creator), Vishnu (the Sustainer), and Shiva (the Destroyer). The Hindu Trinity preceded the Christian Trinity by centuries, and now that we know the degree of trade and exchange of religious information between India and Alexandria, Egypt, we can now recognize the Hindu Trinity influenced the formulation of the Christian Trinity.

Both God the Father and Brahma are cast as the Creator. Brahma, however, does not have the following in the East that God the Father has in the West. There are few temples to Brahma in India, probably because his primary function of creation is past. He is somewhat irrelevant. Brahma does not play the role as lawgiver, nor is He active with the world or the sponsor of a chosen people. Brahma is not to be confused with Brahman, who is the One God of Hinduism, or with the Brahmins, who make up the educated priestly caste of Hinduism.

Vishnu is the second person of the Hindu Trinity. Vishnu is that divine Person of God who incarnates as a human being for some important purpose, generally to defeat evil but also to show us "the Way." The incarnations of Vishnu in the Hindu tradition include Shiva, Ram, and Krishna, and most include Jesus as the Word, also. In some ways, Jesus is more highly esteemed by the populous in India than in, say, New York City. The Wisdom Mother also incarnates and takes flesh in the Hindu system.

What makes the comparison between Krishna and Jesus even more interesting is Vishnu is considered to be the "Word of God" whose job it is to maintain the order of the universe. His job is to turn all things towards good, even if He has to incarnate and take on a human form in order to kill a demon King.

As the third member of the Hindu Trinity, *Shiva the Destroyer,* is quite energetic, but He isn't the Holy Spirit. But in Hinduism there is the adage, "Where there is Shiva there is Shakti," and Shakti is Hinduism's Holy Spirit. I expect Shakti, the Holy Spirit in India, turned into Sophia, the Holy Spirit of the Wisdom books of the Bible because She was much more attractive than the image of God as "the Destroyer." This nomenclature brings to mind a wrestling superhero who beats up bad guys. The destruction in nature is awesome, but to me it is something you want to stay away from. Sophia is very attractive and inviting. I would note Sophia as Holy Spirit adds balance to the overly male, overly aggressive, and authoritarian leaning Christian Trinity.

Pythagoras' School of Philosophy

Upon his return to the West, Pythagoras established his institution of higher learning in Italy (not Greece). Generally, we call these philosophical institutions "schools" and regard them to be something like our secular, liberal universities. Pythagoras's school, however, was nothing like the colleges or universities we have today. It was much more like a monastery or ashram. First, everyone who joined the group gave their property to the commons. They had no individual property, nothing they could call their own. Everything was shared as if they were a family. This is still an ideal in monastic communities where monks and nuns give up their old lives and property and live lives devoted to God.

Pythagoras's followers were vegetarians; they did not eat meat. Then, as now, the reason that Hindus and Buddhists do not eat meat is because they recognize animals to be sentient – conscious and aware beings. Accordingly, the moral rule of *ahimsa* or non-harm is applied to animals as well as humans.

Pythagoras's followers, known as Pythagoreans, practiced monastic silence, sometimes for years. Silence is listening and watching. Silence does not permit impulsive decisions. Silence is also a form of meditation. If we are silent, we are in the present, watching our minds.

The Pythagoreans believed in reincarnation, which we translate as "transmigration of souls." In this after-life conceptualization, people sometimes reincarnated as human, others as animals, depending on their accumulated karma. Plato is generally given credit for giving Christians the concept of "the soul," but you need a soul to have reincarnation, and I expect that Pythagoras, who came before Plato, learned about both souls and reincarnation in India.

We have forgotten about all this, the influence of philosophy and India on the good mystical parts of Jewish and Christian Theology. It seems that early in Christianity's infancy, philosophy and Christianity split. It seems to be over the same argument that divided Mary Magdalene and St. Peter in the Gospel of Mary Magdalene. Mary argued the goal of Jesus' Christianity was to know God intimately, form an Eternal relationship with God; St. Peter wanted to form a new Jewish political reform party. But I expect the divide was aggravated more by class relations, that philosophers thought they were higher, more intelligent than the Christian rabble, who now regarded themselves as inheritors of political society. But all the rudiments of Christian theology from sacraments to the Christology of the Word of God come from the Greeks and "Pagan" Hindus.

Chapter Six: *Alexander the Great*

Enlightened Yogis of India Confront Alexander: "God Abhors War"

Rudyard Kipling once famously wrote, "East is East, and West is West, and never the twain shall meet." This was quite ironic as Kipling made his statement during the British occupation of India. How can we not call the British occupation of India "a meeting" of societies? Perhaps Kipling meant there was some vital element of culture, morality, or religion the two sides could not agree on. To find out more what this difference between East and Western looks like historically in religion and politics, let us examine the history of an earlier, but very important, meeting between India and the West.

The East Has Met the West Many Times

In reality, the East and West have met numerous times, if not continuously for the last 10,000 years. We remember that "Indo-European" is a family of languages that includes Latin, Greek, and Sanskrit. Early religions from India and Europe all featured major warrior deities who hurled terrifying thunderbolts. Animal sacrifice was practiced in the Vedic India as at the Temple in Jerusalem. I would also note that the same war-chariot technology used by King David in the

Bible and throughout ancient history by the Egyptians, Greeks, Persians, Assyrians, and the Romans was the same chariot and bow technology used by Arjuna in the Bhagavad Gita.

Humans have traveled and traded over the seas and oceans from around the tip of India, across the Arabian Sea, up the Red Sea, into the Mediterranean, and all the way across and around Gibraltar to Great Britain, in whole or in part, for millennia. Few Christians realize that the oldest continuously existing Christian church is in Kerala, India, where St. Thomas the Apostle travelled following Jesus' crucifixion.

Alexander the Great and His Conquest

Western history books from ancient times to the present record the story of Alexander the Great's conquest across the Mideast all the way into India, or at least what is now Pakistan. Ever since his rule, Alexander the Great has inspired Western publicists and historians to argue for his greatness. Plutarch (45-127 AD), the Roman historian, featured Alexander in his classic *Histories of Great Men*. When the Guttenberg press was invented, a French version of Plutarch's "Histories" was the second work off the press right after the Bible. In a sense, we could say the Bible and Plutarch's Histories were regarded as the pillars of Western society. Later, Plutarch's version sparked a mythical and enchanted version of Alexander's life called *The Romance of Alexander the Great* in which Alexander performs miracles and thus becomes not just a great historical figure but a super-hero, even a "god." In modern times, we see heavy coffee table books featuring his warrior likeness charging on horseback towards his enemies. Perhaps this is one of our problems. The politicians of the West regard themselves to be the inheritors of Alexander's tradition of greatness demonstrated by his conquest of less informed cultures and races. Alexander the Great became the ideal model of a Western ruler. He was educated by Aristotle, and inspired by the great poetry of Homer, and conquered his way to India. Here is a sample of the Western version of the Alexander the Great's conquest from "Classical Greece," part of the Time/Life Library series:

> Originally his purpose had been simply to destroy the Persian Army. Before long he had decided to take over the whole Persian Empire. And he went on to achieve this aim without losing a single battle. Of all the great generals of the ancient world, Alexander was surely the greatest. He possessed an almost clairvoyant insight into strategy and was a consummately resourceful tactician. Like Napoleon, he believed in swiftness and movement, but he could be patient too, as he showed in his long siege of the formidable fortress of Tyre.
>
> Time/Life: Classical Greece (16)

It is interesting to me that most Western versions assume Alexander's conquest was justified because "he won." There is not mention of the defeated and dead, the wounded, no condemnation of their murder or the suffering of the widows and orphans. Because the Greeks held themselves to be culturally and morally superior, they felt they improved the old society by conquering it and making it more like theirs. An internet literary site makes this observation of Plutarch's work.

> The most important theme (one might say: Plutarch's vision on Alexander's significance in world history) is that

he brought civilization to the barbarians and made them human...

Article on Ancient History (17)

This is an important concept that seems to drive conquests: They think they improve another society because they are ruled by Alexander the Great, rather than the guy who lost because he wasn't good enough, was evil, or had an argument with Alexander about being ruled. In Roman times, great conquests demonstrated, "the glory of Rome," how great it was compared to others because of its economic and military power. After they were conquered, the defeated nation became a colony of Rome, paid tribute to Rome, and were ruled and taxed by Roman governors. The conquered were more likely to end up slaves and laborers for their new rulers, and the dead, widows, and orphans had no voices.

The Eastern View of Alexander's Conquests

The Eastern version of Alexander's conquest is entirely different. Here is an Indian historian's secular analysis of Alexander's invasion:

> Alexander the Great's Indian adventure, though a subject of abiding interest to generations of classically-educated European historians, is not generally an episode on which historians of Indian nationality bother to dwell. They rightly note that it "made no impression historically or politically on India," and that "not even a mention of Alexander is to be found in any of the older India sources.... There is nothing to distinguish his raid in Indian history except 'perfidious massacres' and 'wanton cruelty

> ... and it can hardly be called a great military success as the only military achievements to his credit were the conquest of some petty tribes and states by installment." Alexander's great achievement was not invading India but getting there.
>
> India, A History (18)

"Perfidious massacres" and "wanton cruelty"? I thought Alexander was just and benevolent and was improving society? Would Alexander, the noble ruler, massacre women and children?

Alexander's conquests were recorded in fine detail by his publicists, who traveled with his army to document his "great deeds." Here is a summary of later battles and subsequent massacres.

> When the Chieftain of Massaga fell in battle, the supreme command of the army went to his old mother, Cleophis, who also stood determined to defend her motherland to the last extremity. The example of Cleophis assuming the supreme command of the military also brought the entire population of women of the locality into the fighting. Alexander was only able to reduce Massaga by resorting to political stratagem and actions of betrayal. According to Curitius, "Not only did Alexander slaughter the entire population of Massaga, but also did he reduce its buildings to rubble. A similar slaughter then followed at Ora, another stronghold of the Assakenoi."
>
> Alexander the Great, Wikipedia (19)

It is interesting that the women rallied to the cause, as they would have been part of the conqueror's booty. Alexander loved Homer and was famous for taking a copy of "The Iliad" with him on his conquest. The Iliad starts with the argument between the King and Achilles as to who gets the most beautiful woman in the city they just conquered. The prizes of ancient conquests were the looting of a country's court and treasury – tribute paid to their new ruler – and women, with the women being the real motivator. My guess is that women fought because they did not relish their fate if taken by Alexander's warriors and decided to defend themselves. I would also note that the women being considered to be booty in war is a cause of their status as marital property and lower in caste than warriors in imperial society. Note Alexander's frustration at not getting his prize.

Eastern historians note that Alexander the Great conquered his way into what is now Pakistan, not India, and the cities he conquered were referred to as "tribes," perhaps similar to the "tribes of Israel." Alexander retreated before crossing the Ganges because he likely feared they would never see home again after hearing the kings of the Ganderites and Praesii had rallied "eighty thousand horsemen, two hundred thousand footmen, eight thousand chariots, and six thousand fighting elephants." (21) When confronted by superior forces, Alexander's conquest ended without reaching his goal of crossing over the entirety of India to its eastern shores.

Alexander the Great and the Brahmin Yogis of India

Another, more spiritual, Indian perspective of Alexander was provided by a Western scholar of Indian history, Dr. J. W. McCrindle.

> Upon entering the Western frontiers of the land of the Indus, Alexander sent one of his ministers to find their

leaders in order to agree to the ancient ultimatum – agree to our Greek rule or be conquered. The minister was directed to a yogic sage with whom the following dialog took place.

"Hail to thee, O teacher of the Brahmins!" Onesikritos (Alexander's diplomat) said after seeking out Dandamis in his forest retreat. "The son of the mighty God Zeus, being Alexander who is the Sovereign Lord of all men, asks you to go to him. If you comply, he will reward you with great gifts; if you refuse, he will cut off your head!"

Dandamis received calmly this fairly compulsory invitation, and did not so much as lift up his head from his couch of leaves. "I also am a son of Zeus, if Alexander be such," he commented. "I want nothing that is Alexander's for I am content with what I have, while I see that he wanders with his men over sea and land for no advantage, and is never coming to an end of his wanderings."

This is a masterful argument. It is Alexander who is "poor" because he is wandering in "want." He is not satisfied with his life; Alexander is thus in poverty. Dandamis continues:

"Go tell Alexander that God the Supreme King is never the Author of insolent wrong, but is the Creator of light, of peace, of life, of water, of the body of man and of souls; He receives all men when death sets them free, being then in no way subject to evil disease. He also is the God of my homage, who abhors slaughter and instigates no wars."

We stop here to note the importance of this statement in the face of Alexander's military aggression. God abhors war. Note the parallel with Hosea's words: "God wants compassion, not sacrifices," where sacrifices are the dead in war.

> "Alexander is no god, since he must taste death," continued the sage Dandamis in quiet scorn. "How can one such as he be the world's master when he has not yet seated himself on a throne of inner universal domination? Neither as yet has he entered living into Hades, nor does he even know the course of the sun over the vast regions of this earth. Most nations have not so much as heard his name!
>
> "The gifts Alexander promises are useless to me," Dandamis went on. "The things I prize and find of real worth are trees, which are my shelter, blooming plants, which provide my daily food, and water, which assuages my thirst. Possessions amassed with anxious thought are wont to prove ruinous to those who gather them, causing only the sorrow and vexation that afflict all unenlightened men. As for me, I lie upon forest leaves, and having nothing to guard, close my eyes in tranquil slumber; whereas, had I anything of worldly value, that burden would banish sleep. The earth supplies me with everything I need, even as a mother provides her child with milk. I go wherever I please, unencumbered by material cares.
>
> "Should Alexander cut off my head, he cannot also destroy my soul. My head, then silent, and my body, like a torn garment, will remain on the earth, from which their

elements are taken. I then, becoming Spirit, shall ascend to God. He enclosed us all in flesh and put us on earth to prove whether, when here below, we shall live obedient to His ordinances; and He will require of us, when we depart hence, an account of our lives. He is the Judge of all wrongdoing; the groans of the oppressed ordain the punishment of the oppressor.

"Let Alexander terrify with threats men who wish for wealth and who dread death. Against the Brahmins his weapons are powerless; we neither love gold nor fear death. Go then and tell Alexander this: Dandamis has no need of aught that is yours, and therefore will not go to you; and, if you want anything from Dandamis, come you to him."

Onesikritos duly conveyed the message; Alexander listened with close attention, and felt a stronger desire than ever to see Dandamis; who, though old and naked, was the only antagonist in whom he, the conqueror of many nations had met more than his match.

Autobiography of a Yogi (22)

Alexander later met Dandamis under Dandamis's conditions. Alexander seems to have enjoyed his meeting as he formed a relationship with the Brahmin yogis in the region. He invited a number of Brahmin, ascetics noted for their understanding of philosophy, to answer riddles. Alexander took an enlightened yogi master, Swami Sphines, called "Kalanos" by the Greeks, as an advisor. Some argue Kalanos served as Alexander's spiritual guide or teacher, even guru. However, Alexander's

Greek publicists made Kalanos seem more as a bother. But based on the following story, Kalanos impressed Alexander's army.

> The sage Kalanos accompanied Alexander to Persia. On a stated day, at Susa in Persia, Kalanos gave up his aged body by entering a funeral pyre in view of the whole Macedonian army. The historians record the astonishment of the soldiers as they observed that the yogi had no fear of pain or death; he never once moved from his position as he was consumed in flames. Before leaving for his cremation, Kalanos had embraced many of his close companions, but had refrained from bidding farewell to Alexander, to whom the Hindu sage had merely remarked, "I shall see you in Babylon." Alexander left Persia and, a year later, died in Babylon.
>
> Autobiography of a Yogi (22)

There are also East Indian stories of Alexander the Great in a different genre – the Indian religious folk story. As Hindus see life from the perspective of karma, that you will reap what you sow, their stories often have a moral lesson to them. Among the most popular of these "fables" are those of Alexander's last wishes.

> On the way back from his conquest of the East, Alexander took the more difficult route and became terminally ill. While on his deathbed he longed for his mother and home, but he knew he would die before he got there. In despair of his life, Alexander called his generals and told them, "I have

three wishes. Please carry them out all three without fail after I die." His generals agreed and listened intently.

"My first desire is that my coffin be carried by my physicians alone. Secondly, the path leading to the graveyard must be paved with all the jewels and precious stones which I have gathered during my conquests. My third last wish is that you cut holes in the coffin so that my arms dangle out of it when I am buried."

His generals were perplexed and asked Alexander to explain his strange requests. "We assure you that your wishes will be fulfilled, but please tell us the reasoning of your strange requests." Alexander replied, "I would like the world to benefit from the lessons I have just learned. With my first wish, I want people to know that no physicians can save anybody from death whose time has come. My second wish is to tell people that all my life I chased after wealth and spent my life yearning after riches, which are now worthless to me. I can take them no further. And with my last wish, I want the people to know that I came empty handed into this world and will leave this world empty handed."

Anonymous, Indian Oral Tradition

The oral tradition of the Indian folktale still exists. This is my version of multiple versions I have heard both at Hindu gatherings and read on the internet. Generally, these stories are told at religious gatherings as entertaining teachings. There is no standard version that I know of. Best put it in the "Anonymous" classification so anyone can use this story for instruction as it was intended.

Western sources report Alexander's death was sudden; he was probably poisoned. So this scene of Alexander describing three wishes is unlikely. But as with many legendary scenes that may or may not have actually occurred, they serve as moral guides, and these Indian folktales sound surprisingly Christian.

In this story above, Alexander realizes the error of his ways. We hear echoes of Ecclesiasticus: "Vanity, vanity, all is vanity." All his wealth and all his glory are of no use to him now as he meets death. Alexander cannot take his wealth with him, and he faces death, the final accountant.

Do not store up treasures for yourself on earth, where moths and woodworm destroy them, and thieves [metaphors for time and death] break in and steal them. But store up treasure for yourselves in heaven.... For where your treasure is, there will your heart be also.

You cannot serve two masters, God and money.
Matthew 6:19-21,24

The Great Transformation

Now for the plot thickener: In her book *The Great Transformation*, Karen Armstrong advances the historical model that the emergence of the great religions occurred as a spiritual response to the suffering and brutal savagery of war. We also believe that this "Great Transformation" is actually a historical dialectic of substantial religious and spiritual importance in which humankind takes its next step in its evolution, or doesn't. And here, on the border of India, we see the dialectic of Enlightenment and compassion or war and conquests take voice in Dandamis' words:

> Go tell Alexander that God the Supreme King is never the Author of insolent wrong, but is the Creator of light, of peace, of life, of water, of the body of man and of souls; He receives all men when death sets them free, being then in no way subject to evil disease. He also is the God of my homage, who abhors slaughter and instigates no wars.
>
> Autobiography of a Yogi

Is Dandamis' statement not a spiritual reaction against war? Did the yogis not win the argument concerning the nature of God and human beings?

This Yogi speaks with conviction about the wondrous nature of his God in declarative sentences, thus we tend to believe him. God is the creator of all things good, of light and nature, of life and water. We worship the God of life rather than a god of war and death.

But then you think about it and wonder, *How does this guy know what he is talking about? How does this scantily clad, long-haired "Mr. Natural" know what God wants or doesn't want? How do we even know God is real?*

Chapter Seven: *Library of Alexandria*

How Septuagint Met the Upanishads in Alexandria, Egypt

This chapter of our history of Biblical scripture begins as Alexander the Great's quest ends. Alexander's troops, weary of conquering, long for home. Alexander divides his army into two groups, one returning by land, the other by sea. Alexander led his men on the more difficult desert route as the ideal Stoic leader should and died on the way back in 323 BCE on the desert plains of Babylon as foretold by the yogi, Swami Sphines.

He may have died from festering old wounds. He had many, one from a spear that pierced his lungs. He may have also been poisoned by one of his generals or servants. He died after a bout of copious drinking. His end, which is endlessly debated, was not particularly "glorious."

In the division of Alexander's empire, Ptolemy I (Philadelphus), Alexander's childhood friend and confidant, received the choicest kingdom, which included much of the Middle East, including the Holy Land and the breadbasket of the Mediterranean, Egypt. Ptolemy ruled from Alexandria, Egypt – the Mediterranean port city sitting on the western edge of the Nile Delta that Alexander established before he left on his military adventure.

Ptolemy brought the storied legend of Alexander the Great home to Alexandria along with Alexander's body. Scholars say that by claiming Alexander's body, Ptolemy laid claim to Alexander's great heritage.

Alexander was "Great" and Ptolemy would rule in the tradition of Alexander's glory and greatness.

The Great Library of Alexandria

The Great City, the Great Library, and the great Lighthouse of Alexandria were and are still famous. The library was not a collection of books but a complex comparable to a cosmopolitan university with an attached museum, lecture halls, and courts for small group discussions. With a truly international port and the great library, Alexandria became the meeting place of scholars from around the world. It became a mixing pot of eastern and western philosophies with Buddhist monks, Brahmin priests, and yogis mixing with philosophers, Jewish lovers of Sophia (philosophers), and budding young rabbis mixing, discussing common interests, and defining who God was to them.

Because of the Library of Alexandria's scholarly tradition, its wealth, and the industry of the teachers and librarians, Alexandria remained an important intellectual center of religious thought throughout the early history of Christianity. At the Nicene Council six centuries later, both the key actors, both Athanasius and Arius, had roots in Alexandria. Even after the Council of Nicaea, most of the theologians advancing Christianity were tied to Greek philosophy through Alexandria. Basil the Great traveled to Alexandria, and his friend and fellow Cappadocian Father Gregory of Naziansus studied there. Later, we will see how Basil saved the Holy Spirit and much of Jesus' teachings in the now institutionalized Church.

The great Lighthouse of Alexandria became an important landmark in history, one of the "Seven Wonders of the Ancient World." The great fires streaming light upwards must have been a wondrous and welcome sight for night travelers from the East as they sailed south and west along the coast using the cool prevailing winds off the Mediterranean Sea. Through the ages, the lighthouse has come to symbolize the "enlightening" flame of knowledge and wisdom that the library has long represented for Egypt, Western civilization, and the world.

Buying Books from Around the World for the Library

Ptolemy I inaugurated the Great Library of Alexandria, but it was Ptolemy II (Soter) who actually built and stocked the library with books. Ptolemy II understood the importance of knowledge of history and law, legends and myth, religion and theology – the power the written word had on people. To acquire books for the library, he opened up the Egyptian treasury to buy books about how people lived and thought, especially about religion and politics.

Opening the Egyptian treasury to buying and eventually producing books was one of the most important imperial government decisions of all time. Ptolemy's investment catalyzed a wave of demand for books and manuscripts that sent their value skyrocketing. Abundant money had merchants of books vying around the world for new titles. In Egypt visiting ships were rudely ransacked by resellers looking for more books to meet the demand.

Alexandria's Ties to Ashoka the Great in India

Alexander the Great conquered his way to the borders of India, but ultimately failed in his goal and had to turn back home. Through diplomacy, Ptolemy II opened up relations with Ashoka, also known as Ashoka the Great. He was the famous Buddhist Emperor of India (268-232 BCE), who is given credit for uniting the Indian subcontinent and promoting Buddhism across ancient Asia. One of the reasons that Alexander's conquest was so "great" was that his armies traveled so many thousands of miles overland. The sea route to India from Egypt was well-established millennia earlier.

Ashoka the Great

As many Western histories begin with Alexander the Great, many in the East begin with Ashoka the Great. The comparison is fascinating. Ashoka waged a particularly destructive conquest against the state of Kalinga, which he conquered in about 260 BCE. Afterwards, he realized the suffering and waste he had caused and converted to Buddhism. Ashoka confessed that he had waged the war out of his ego's desire to rule and conquer and that as a result of his actions more than 100,000 human beings had died. Ashoka is remembered for erecting the *Ashoka Pillars,* for spreading his edicts sponsoring Buddhist compassion and non-violence, for sending Buddhist monks to Sri Lanka and Central Asia, and for establishing monuments marking several significant sites in the life of Gautama Buddha. (23)

Ashoka is famous for being a great general, a great conqueror, and then, after seeing all the suffering he caused from his conquest, repenting, converting to Buddhism, and actively and successfully promoting unity and peace in the region through the practice of Buddhism. Ashoka provides us with an excellent example of a personal "Great Transformation" of a ruler reacting spiritually to the suffering of others caused by a war he initiated and committing himself to peace and repentance. The inscription on one of Ashoka's stupas (commemorative monument) states:

> This religious inscription has been engraved in order that our sons and grandsons may not think a new conquest is necessary; that they may not think conquest by the sword deserves the name of conquest; that they may see in it nothing but destruction and violence...
>
> Autobiography of Yogi (24)

Note that realizing you are causing others pain in war, admitting you did wrong is hard on the ego. What did it take so that Ashoka was driven to repent? The Wisdom books of the Bible offer some insight. "Fear of God is the beginning of Wisdom."

The Book Buyers Besiege India

Perhaps based on his father's memories of Alexander and his army's meetings and discussions with the Brahmin Yogis, Ptolemy II's book buying interests extended into India. There, in the Far East, we find a story that tells us much about how the people of India regarded their sacred literature at that time.

> A Greek merchant came to a temple priest to purchase a rare religious manuscript that told how a person could gain immortality. After some negotiation they reached an agreement. "Come back tomorrow morning, and I will have the manuscript prepared for you," The priest said. The buyer agreed. He came back the following morning just in time to see the last sheets of the document he purchased slide into the fire. The priest, having just spoken the last

words contained in the document to his son, turned to the purchaser. "Here is your document. My son will go with you. He has memorized every word."

Anonymous: Indian Oral Tradition

Even Eastern scholars criticize the ancient Hindu priests for maintaining the oral tradition for as long as they did rather than writing it down. But knowing by memory the words of rites and scripture guaranteed you a job of some importance at the temple. It made you special. Putting religious songs, poetry, and myth in writing detached them from their more spiritual and devotional context in temple worship and the intimacy of knowing a passage by heart.

Isn't it interesting that the book buyer was looking for a rare book on how to find immortality, translated in our Bibles as Eternal Life? Was that what the book buyers were looking for, the path to Eternal Life?

Ptolemy II Commissioned the Production of the Old Testament

In perhaps the most important confluence of events in Western history, Ptolemy II also commissioned the writing and publishing of the Old Testament of the Judeo-Christian Bible. He commissioned 72 Jewish scholars, six from each of the 12 tribes of Israel, to write a history of their people. The Greek Septuagint is named after the 72 scholars and is the basis for the Orthodox Old Testament we use today.

When I was in high school, I was taught that the Jewish scholars translated the Hebrew Old Testament into Greek. The problem is there was no "Old Testament" sitting around before they published it. The 72 scholars "produced" the Septuagint Old Testament in a process of identifying, buying, collecting, selecting, editing, compiling, and translating regional stories and Jewish religious and legal texts into Greek. The scholars who finally wrote down the final copy were of the Jewish intellectual class, who spoke and wrote in Greek, and as turns out, thought in Greek.

At that time, the Greek-speaking population of Jews in Alexandria was as large as in Jerusalem. The editors of my Bible note that some of the sayings in Proverbs came from Arab as well as Jewish sources. I don't know, however, how they differentiated Arab from Jew before the Old Testament was written, as both Arab and Jew claim they descended from Abraham. And some of the stories and Proverbs are from Arab lands and authors.

How the Septuagint Met the Upanishads in Alexandria Egypt

So now we know how Sophia was enshrined in the Judeo-Christian Bible: She was put there intentionally by Hellenized, Greek-speaking Jewish lovers of Sophia.

Solomon, the wisest of Jews, exclaimed his love for Sophia in the book of Wisdom. As Solomon loved Sophia and spoke in the Greek vocabulary, Solomon was a great example of a Jewish lover of Sophia, a Jewish philosopher. In many ways, I think the Wisdom books attributed to Solomon are perhaps the best existent description of philosophical religious practice, including meditation, sacramental rites, and devotion to God. I expect they also believed in reincarnation and karma. According to many, evidence in the Bible shows Jesus did also.

The Upanishads Met the Septuagint in Alexandria and Brought Forth Christianity

It was in the halls of the great library that philosophers, Jewish rabbis, Brahmin yogis, and Buddhist monks met, read each other's books, shared their spiritual knowledge, and discussed the eternal questions of the purpose of life and what happens after death. The mixing of Eastern and Western religious concepts was essential to the formulation of the Wisdom Movement and eventually early Christianity. It was at the Library of Alexandria that the writers of the Septuagint Old Testament met the wisdom of the Upanishads and brought forth the Wisdom books of the Bible, the Wisdom Movement, and eventually Christianity.

Chapter Eight: *The Prophets*

The Prophet's Rebellion and the Great Transformation

It is in the prophetic books of the Bible that Dr. Karen Armstrong says the "Great Transformation" occurred. To review, her concept of this transformation is that religious movements are formed based on a spiritual reaction to the suffering and death caused by war.

> When they started to look for the causes of violence in the psyche, the axial philosophers penetrated their inner world and began to explore a hitherto undiscovered realm of human expression.
>
> The consensus of the Axial Age is an eloquent testimony to the unanimity of the spiritual quest of the human race. The Axial peoples all found that the compassion ethic worked. All the great traditions that were created at this time are in agreement about the supreme importance of charity and benevolence, and this tells us something important about our humanity.
>
> The Great Transformation (25)

I would agree that the Great Transformation in the Judeo-Christian tradition begins with the publishing of the prophetic books, gets developed in the Wisdom books of the Old Testament and is reinforced and verified as "the Way, the Truth, and the Life" by Jesus Christ in the New Testament. I would simply note that Dr. Armstrong didn't have to go back to the seventh and eighth centuries BCE, the "axial age," to find wars and violence against which to revolt. It was not as if wars and conquests ended during the axial age in the Middle East. There were plenty of wars and bloodshed right there in Alexandria, Egypt, when and where the 72 scholars published the Old Testament.

Although Ptolemy II built the library and is generally considered the best of the Ptolemaic emperors, the Pentateuch and the history books were officiated over by later rulers of the dynasty. The dynasty as a whole was extremely violent, tyrannical, and fratricidal. In order to understand the Bible, you have to understand the times it was written in, and they were not good times and the Ptolemies were not nice people. The Ptolemaic Dynasty was famous not only for its cast of characters, including Cleopatra, but for the violence of their rule.

> Over the generation, the family indulged in what has been termed "an orgy of pillage and murder," lurid even by colorful Macedonian standards. It was not an easy clan in which to distinguish one's self, but Ptolemy IV did, at the height of the empire. In the late third century he murdered his uncle, brother, and mother. Courtiers saved him from poisoning his wife by doing so themselves, once she had produced an heir. Over and over mothers sent troops against sons. Sisters waged war against brothers. Cleopatra's great grandmother fought one civil war against her parents, a second against her children. No one

> suffered as acutely as the inscribers of monuments, left
> to contend with the near-simultaneous inaugurations and
> assassinations....
>
> Cleopatra, a Life (26)

Surely this imperial dynasty would be considered representative of the more negative side of our dialectic of what God doesn't want: sacrifices and holocausts. The problem is the values and laws of the imperial Ptolemaic Dynasty are written into parts of the Bible. It was the laws, authoritarian rule, and the imperial culture of the Ptolemaic Dynasty and their servile high priest that the prophets were rebelling against.

Perhaps the writers of the prophetic books took incidents from the past, but based on the subsequent history the prophet's criticism was directed to their contemporaries: The Ptolemaic Dynasty and the high priests knew the criticism was aimed at them, and they didn't like it.

The Prophetic Transformation

In the prophetic books there is a dramatic change in tone from the earlier Pentateuch and historical books. Rather than saying how great their religious leaders, rulers, and patriarchs were, the prophets berated their rulers for doing evil rather than good. In Isaiah, we hear God's total frustration with the way the Jewish rulers are governing Israel:

> I am sick of holocausts of rams and the fat of calves.
> The blood of bulls and goats revolts me.
> Who asked you to trample over my courts?
> Bring me your worthless offerings no more,
> The smoke of them fills me with disgust....

> Take your wrong-doing out of my sight.
>
> Cease to do evil.
>
> Learn to do good,
>
> Search for justice,
>
> Help the oppressed,
>
> Be just to the orphan,
>
> Plead for the widow.
>
> Isaiah 1:11-13, 16-17

The radical nature of God's complaint against His own priests (!) is built into the language Isaiah uses. God is "sick" of them. God tells them directly, "Go away from me." In ancient Judaism, sacrifices were meant to please or at least appease God. Now, their sacrifices make God sick? Something has changed.

Then the God of the prophets links sacrifice to violence done to others ("your hands are covered with blood") and tells them to stop doing evil and start doing good. Again, God is quite direct:

> Your hands are covered with blood,
>
> Wash, make yourself clean.
>
> Take your wrong-doing out of my sight.
>
> Isaiah 1:16-17

What God Wants

If God doesn't want sacrifices and holocausts, what does God want? In a transformational passage, the prophet Hosea tells us exactly what God wants.

> God wants compassion, not sacrifices.
>
> God wants [intimate Knowledge of God], not holocausts.
>
> Hosea 6:6

These lines from Hosea are actually quite famous and often quoted. In fact, Jesus uses them when He and His disciples are accosted by the Pharisees for gathering food on the Sabbath: "And if you had understood the meaning of the words: 'What I want is mercy, not sacrifices,' you would not have condemned the blameless." (Matthew 12:7).

It is interesting that in Matthew, my Jerusalem Bible uses the translation from the King James Bible, "I want mercy." But in Hosea the same lines are translated as "I want love." But I am thinking that whereas wanting mercy might appeal to rulers and judges, the love translation is much more radical: God "wants love, not sacrifices." Isn't that the Greatest Commandment: To love God and our neighbor as our Self? But how is love active in giving mercy, forgiving another? I prefer to compromise between the two words "love" and "mercy" with a translation of "compassion" based on our knowledge of your own humanity.

But it is the second line that is central to our thesis. Here God wants "knowledge of God." I think the wording is off *What, God doesn't know Himself? I thought He was all knowing, and here He doesn't even know who He is?* This is humorous, but wrong. It turns out that God wants to have Communion with us, for us to have intimate knowledge of God. Dr. Armstrong explains:

> As he makes Yahweh say: "What I want is love (*besed*), not sacrifice; knowledge of God (*daath Elohim*), not holocausts. He did not mean theological knowledge: the word *daath*

comes from the verb *yada*: to know, which has sexual connotations. Thus J says that Adam "knew" his wife, Eve.

A History of God (27)

What Dr. Armstrong is describing is intimate knowledge indeed, and we will use that translation and say God wants "intimate knowledge of God, not holocausts." This line works well in the context of the romantic and sexual tension built up between Lover and Beloved in the Song of Songs. Later we will see that the St. Paul who wrote Ephesians asks the Holy Spirit to bless us with "full knowledge of God," which is the same as "intimate knowledge of God." Other translations of this mystical concept include Enlightenment, Samadhi, Gnosis, Baptism, Rebirth in the Holy Spirit, and Union-Communion with God.

The Septuagint Publishing Company Scholars Go Independent

In 126 BCE, Ptolemy VIII became violently upset and expelled all the "intellectuals" (28) from the city, which is a pretty harsh reaction in a city built on scholarship and priding in cosmopolitan thinking. Some intellectuals were apparently killed for their writings, perhaps because of their criticism of their imperial rulers and high priests. At the same time, the financial commission that had been responsible for the production of the Old Testament, ended. The Ptolemaic Dynasty broke with their publishing company.

I expect the complaints and judgments of the prophets against their priests and rulers angered the authoritarian and brutal King of the Ptolemaic Dynasty. Despite the Dynasty's violent criticism of their work, the Septuagint Publishing Company moved to a more isolated location further outside Alexandria and kept producing books for the Jewish room at the Great Library of Alexandria and for special customers who could afford their own hand-copied document documenting the greatness of their religion and race. Publishing the Old Testament was a very popular, financially secure, and influential business. They kept on publishing but with a prophetic voice telling us what God wants, not what the Ptolemies want.

Chapter Nine: *Proverbs*

Sophia's Instruction Manual on How to Find Her

Sophia makes Her first appearance in the Old Testament book of Proverbs. The book contains a collection of proverbs gleaned from a variety of regional sources, plus an introduction in which the narrator, a father counseling his son (we'll call him Solomon), introduces Hagia Sophia, Holy Wisdom. This introduction, lasting nine chapters, explains the goal of life and the methodology by which we seek and find God.

The book of Proverbs is an Old Testament favorite studied in Bible schools and theology departments throughout Christendom. It lays the foundation of the Wisdom vocabulary of mystically based "words of deep meaning," metaphors, and the parable streams that Jesus uses, as well as the Christian sacramental system. Proverbs is an early instruction guide on how to know God. Jesus empowered Sophia's methods, so they are still available today if we properly understand their intent.

The collection of proverbs is regional coming from both Arab and Hebrew sources. Many may be ancient and some are ascribed to King Solomon. Many of the proverbs are insightful and witty. The reader is invited to peruse them, but here we will focus on Sophia, the protagonist of the book.

Sophia appears in the introduction to the book of Proverbs. The influence of Greek philosophy is evident. The introduction to Proverbs features the philosopher's beloved Sophia and many Greek "words of deep meaning," including "the Word" or "Logos," which is Greek in origin.

The heading atop the first chapter of Proverbs in my Bible is, "Title and Purpose of the book." It reads as follows:

> For learning what Wisdom and discipline are,
> For understanding words of deep meaning,
> For acquiring an enlightened attitude of mind:
> Virtue, justice, and fair dealing;
> For teaching sound judgment to the ignorant,
> And knowledge and sense to the young.
> For perceiving the meaning of proverbs and obscure sayings,
> The saying of the sages and their riddles.
> Let the wise listen and he will learn yet more,
> And the man of discernment will acquire the art of guidance.
> Fear of Yahweh is the beginning of knowledge;
> Fools spurn Wisdom [Enlightenment] and discipline.
>
> Proverbs 1:2-7

We remember Sophia was introduced in the book of Holy Wisdom as the "Holy Spirit of Instruction." This is essentially Sophia's instruction manual on how to live the life of a lover of Sophia, a philosopher, her devotee. Much of the instruction has to do with changing the way we perceive the world. Sophia tries to change the way we perceive the world by reprogramming how we use language. The idea is that if we change the way we think about God, the universe, our fellow human beings and how to relate to them, we would be able to perceive the world differently, more accurately, and full of wonder. By reprogramming ourselves, we could see reality "in an Enlightened manner," as the Kingdom of God as Jesus later calls it.

The passage above begins by stating the importance of knowing what "Wisdom" is. In the East, "Holy Wisdom" is Enlightenment and is granted by the Wisdom Mother. This experience of Enlightenment provides us with knowledge we did not have before. This experience would include the perception of God and change how we relate to God and our neighbors.

Sophia Teaches the Importance of Discipline

In ancient times, it seems discipline was harsher than today. And, in fact, we do see some "spare the rod, spoil the child" rhetoric in the Wisdom books of the Old Testament. But discipline meant different things to the different philosophical schools. The warrior and ruling castes believed self-discipline to be that element of character that makes you great, raises you above others. Practice and discipline make you a better warrior, and if you aren't a great warrior and got yourself killed because you didn't train hard enough or just weren't lucky. We note this same Stoic philosophy is one of the foundations of capitalist societies. Your success or failure is based on your character. If you are rich, you must be great, and if you are poor, it is your fault.

In the Sophia/Wisdom tradition, the goal of discipline is first to control the mind. Then one can direct the will and effort to go towards the goal. In the Wisdom tradition, the goal is intimate knowledge of God, Enlightenment. Those so directed are not motivated by gold and silver but by "virtue, justice, and fair dealing."

Jesus' Yoke is Easy

But in comparison to the Stoic discipline of the political class, Jesus promoted His discipline as "easy":

> Take my yoke upon you and learn from me,
> For I am gentle and humble of heart; and you will find rest.
> My yoke is easy, and my burden light.
>
> Matthew 11:28-31

It is interesting that Jesus' use of the term "yoke" to describe the kind of discipline He sponsors. "To yoke" is also the root word of Yoga. Given His knowledge of many languages and philosophies He was probably making on pun, actually meaning, "My Yoga is easy." I like this idea of following Jesus' way being "easy" and use the idea throughout the book as encouragement to actually practice.

So why is Jesus' yoke easy? First, you have to differentiate between what Jesus did for Himself and what He wants us to do. He fasted and prayed in the hot desert sun and slept out among the rocks at night. This was hard. He is gentler on us. Jesus' yogic path of evolution towards God emphasized the "Greatest Commandment:" loving God and our neighbors as our Selves, seeking first the Kingdom of God, and doing unto others what we would have them do to us.

Ironically, perhaps the most difficult part of the Greatest Commandment is, "loving your neighbor as your Self." It is difficult to love the jerk weaving in and out of traffic endangering everybody, someone who pokes us in the eye, or tells me I am stupid. I believe it was the Lucy character in *Peanuts* who coined the phrase, "I love mankind; it is people I can't stand." We all have egos, and we like to win. It takes more than good intentions to make life work. It takes a great deal of skill and know-how that we aren't necessarily born with. We all learn along the way. Learning forgiveness is part of Jesus' Way.

Spiritual Practice, Meditation, and Prayer

Philosophers and early Christians prayed and meditated. Praying and meditating are disciplines unto themselves. Both require concentration. Note, you can say prayers fast and get done quickly with no concentration, or you can concentrate on an understanding of the words of the prayer. In meditation you focus your mind on an "image of God" or a mantra (generally a short prayer that you repeat) or perhaps your breath. But after a while, the mind wanders and the meditator needs to re-focus, usually repeatedly. This strengthens the will as well as well absorbing Sophia's grace.

Beginning Zen students often are taught to start meditation practice by simply counting their breaths. They are directed to count ten breaths and then repeat. This sounds easy. Many beginners are surprised that they get lost in thought before they get to four. So you bring the mind back and refocus, and try again and again and again. Focusing the mind and keeping it focused on the image of God, the memory of God's presence is the lifetime direction of a yogi. But I would note that the mind might go more naturally to the image of the glorious Sophia and a mantra telling Her you love Her and adore Her. If you want to meditate on God, and God is glorious, why not meditate on the glory of God, Sophia? The closer you get to God the happier you should be, and "Happy are they who meditate on Sophia."

Why Teach with Parables?

When Jesus started teaching with parables, many did not understand Him. "Where is this Kingdom of God you are talking about?" the scribes and Pharisees, the scholars of Hebrew scripture, would ask. *Why don't you just tell us what you mean instead of speaking in riddles?* Even Jesus' Apostles had trouble understanding what Jesus was saying. He had to take them aside and explain the seed-sowing parable to them in private. Apparently, they were very literal-minded back then, in the Holy Land, and this is the kind of thinking that Sophia in Proverbs is trying to change.

In the first chapter of Proverbs, Jesus' parables would be classified as "perceiving the meaning of ... obscure sayings of the sages and their riddles." "Perceiving" is a key word here, as is the idea that Sophia is the Holy Spirit of Wisdom and Perception. With a change in perception, you see the world differently so we obtain an enlightened frame of mind.

Neither the scribes nor Pharisees nor the Apostles understood His parables. At one point Jesus turns to His questioners and asks them what is wrong with them:

> Have you no perception? Are your minds closed?
> Have you eyes that do not see, ears that do not hear?
>
> Mark 8:18

What "eyes" and "ears" is Jesus is talking about? Here, the Upanishads are helpful in de-coding Jesus' mystical meaning.

> ... Did you ask your teacher for that spiritual Wisdom
> Which enables you to hear the unheard,
> Think the unthought, and know the unknown.
>
> Chandogya Upanishad (29)

Hear the unheard? It sounds almost Zen, like the koan about hearing "the sound of one hand clapping." The purpose of a koan is to perceive the world beyond how it appears literally in day-to-day consciousness, "to see the unseen."

In Proverbs, Solomon repeatedly expounds on the need for clear perception and tells us where we find it. We find it in Sophia.

> ... learn what clear perception is.
> Acquire Sophia, acquire perception,
> Never forget Her, never deviate from my words.
> Love Her,
> She will watch over you.
> The beginning of holy wisdom?
> Acquire Sophia (Wisdom/Enlightenment).
> At all costs of all your treasure, acquire perception.
> Hold Her close, and She will make you great;
> Embrace Her, and She will be your pride;
> She will set a crown of grace on your head,
> Bless you with a glorious diadem.
>
> Proverbs 4:1-9

What is this Wisdom that Sophia provides? What are we to perceive? What is the goal?

> If your plea is for clear perception
> If you cry out for discernment,
> If you look for it as if it were silver
> And search for it as for buried treasure,

> You will then understand what fear of Yahweh is,
>
> And discover Knowledge of God.
>
> Proverbs 2:3-6

Later in Proverbs, Solomon repeats the same.

> The fear of Yahweh is the beginning of Wisdom,
>
> Knowledge of the Holy One is perception indeed.
>
> Proverbs 9:10

So the goal is to have Knowledge of God, of the Holy One, exactly what Hosea says God wants. Right here in Proverbs we have the definition of who we are to seek and find God. After reading about Sophia in the book of Holy Wisdom and of Her role in Songs, we know the Holy One who they sought was Sophia, the Holy Spirit of Wisdom and Perception, thus also God and the Holy One.

Sophia Introduces the Eucharistic Meal

I was surprised when I read in Proverbs that Sophia introduced the Eucharistic meal.

> Come eat my bread,
>
> And drink the wine I have prepared.
>
> Proverbs 9:4-5

This is another of those moments when I wonder, *Why didn't anyone tell me it was Sophia who introduces the Eucharist in the Bible? I thought Jesus instituted the sacrament of Communion, and here Sophia beat Him to it.* It seems the Eucharist meal was celebrated in mystery sects active in Alexandria, Egypt, before, during, and after Jesus' lifetime, although we don't know what words they spoke in their ceremony. There are passages in the Gospel of Thomas that even suggest Jesus was not only active in these sacramental sects but may have been a master at "solving" or interpreting these ritual ceremonies. We aren't supposed to know it, but mystery sects in Alexandria practiced the Eucharistic meal under the auspices of Sophia, and everyone knew it even back then. We don't know exactly what words they said, but as Jesus and Sophia are allied, married and One, we will argue later, I expect they agreed in Communion with God and that we are all a part of the Word's Mystical Body.

Sophia's Words of Deep Meaning

One of the ways Sophia changes our language is that Her vocabulary is filled with new "words of deep meaning." That is, they are based on mystical experience. These words of deep meaning include "the Word," "the Kingdom of God," and "the Self." Rather than doing a long dissertation on the meaning of the Word of God, I am going to do a brief discussion of the evolution of the meaning of the Word of God over time.

The "Word of God" as the Object of Meditation

Where did the "Word of God" originate? It originated in India. We have all seen pictures of yogis meditating alone in caves. Why caves? In addition to providing some shelter, caves are noted for their silence. Yogis sat in the caves and meditated by listening for "the Word of God." It is actually a vibration that some hear, others feel, that permeates through time and space and consciousness.

In the East, the Word of God is the active and holy vibration, indicating the omnipresence of God Consciousness that fills and orders the universe. This vibration gives Life and consciousness to all that live. When experienced, the Word is perceived not to be a thing but a Person. In some systems of yoga, the practitioner is encouraged to chant *Aum (or Ohm)* to teach the student to be aware of spiritual vibration and its impact on the mind. In meditating on *Aum*, the student tunes into an awareness of space in which sound and prayer vibrate, and it is in that prayer space that Sophia appears if you pray to Her, meditate on Her, and love Her when you are ready.

Chapter Ten: *Proverbs*

Sophia Delights God and Plays with the Sons of Man

In the previous chapter we discussed some of Sophia's teachings. In this chapter we will cover Her stagecraft, Her appearances in the book of Proverbs. We will focus on what She is like as a Person. We first meet Sophia as a town crier, preaching to us from the streets:

> Sophia [Wisdom] calls aloud in the streets,
> She raises her voice in the public squares;
> She calls out at the street corners,
> She delivers her message at the city gates,
> "You ignorant people, how much longer will you
> Cling to your ignorance?"
> Since I have called and you have refused me,
> Since I have beckoned and no one has taken notice,
> Since you have ignored all my advice
> And rejected my warnings,
> When calamity bears down on you like a storm
> And your distress is like a whirlwind,
> When disaster and anguish bear down on you,
> Then they shall call to me, but I will not answer.

They shall seek me eagerly and shall not find me.
They spurned all my warnings:
So they must eat the fruits of their own actions
And choke themselves with their own scheming.

Proverbs 1:20-22, 24-28, 30-31

That is quite a sermon, somewhat like the fire and brimstone sermons of old. We almost wonder, *Is this a warning or a threat?* Do we find this Sophia attractive in this scene? For me, She is a bit overbearing. If She is the Holy Spirit of Instruction, what is She teaching here?

She is teaching us "fear of God." An often-repeated axiom of the Wisdom books of the Bible is, "Fear of God is the beginning of Wisdom." It is actually fear of karma. And remember, Jesus turns away from the condemned the same way Sophia does here in Matthew 25 because we didn't recognize Him in others.

I don't believe in *forever hell*, but I do believe in karma, and people find themselves in hellish spots in many situations, often willingly. I think we can work off bad karma by "doing good" and get closer to God by loving God. Or we go away from God through selfish actions that cause painful karmic blowback. Fear of God is a very healthy attitude towards life. In the Wisdom books of the Bible, fear of God is the beginning of wisdom.

The Things God Abhors

In addition to warning us to fear God, Proverbs lists the actions that God abhors:

There are six things that Yahweh hates,
Seven that his soul abhors:

> A haughty look,
>
> A lying tongue,
>
> Hands that shed innocent blood,
>
> A heart that weaves wicked plots
>
> Feet that hurry to do evil,
>
> A false witness who lies with every breath,
>
> A man who sows dissension among brothers.
>
> Proverbs 6:16-19

I would assume that "hands that shed innocent blood" would include those of Alexander the Great and most of the Ptolemies that ruled Egypt. The lives of these were the lives of those God admonished through the prophets. But here, rather than trying to make up, God turns away from them.

Sophia at Creation

Although Sophia is somewhat scary in the first chapter of Proverbs, She changes Her character and personality between scenes and appears at creation, delighting God and playing with the "Sons of Man":

> Yahweh created me
>
> When His purpose first unfolded,
>
> Before the Oldest of His works.
>
> From everlasting I was firmly set
>
> From the beginning,
>
> Before the earth came into being.
>
> The deep was not,
>
> Before I was born.

...
> I was by His side, a master craftsman,
>
> Delighting Him, day after day,
>
> Ever at play in His Presence,
>
> At play everywhere in His world,
>
> Delighting to be with the sons of man.
>
> Proverbs 8:22-24, 30-31

Although later controversial, these lines are a delightful poetic portrayal of Sophia. Sophia delights God and delights "to be with the sons of man." I find Sophia also delights me.

Of all the titles used for Jesus in the New Testament, the "Son of Man" is the most common. As a simple definition, I would say the "Son of Man" in the Old Testament is a prophet. For example, God tells Ezekiel, "Son of Man, prophesy." But being a prophet also means you have a special relationship with God as the Holy Spirit.

In the Nicene Creed, the Holy Spirit "speaks through the prophets." Some argue that the prophets are not the Holy Spirit's megaphone, but then if you have the awesome and all-powerful Holy Spirit within telling you what to say or do, you do it even though there might be some resistance. But rather than overwhelming the poor prophets, Sophia "delights to be" with the Sons of Man, which seems a more enjoyable experience.

The "Seek and Find" Parable Stream Is Developed in Proverbs

The book of Proverbs uses the same "seek and you will find" parable stream mentioned first in the Prophetic books, developed in the Wisdom books of the Bible and then extensively used by Jesus in the New Testament. We remember Jesus directing us to "seek first the Kingdom of God." This is, however, a very abstract idea for most people, and there are few Christians currently looking for this kingdom, mostly because they don't know where to look. Or maybe they think they don't have to look anymore because it is now the post-Messianic Age. But still, even in this twenty-first century, it is our first duty to seek the presence of God in the material world. Once we discover the true nature of the universe, it becomes the Kingdom of God.

The Development of the "Seek and Find" Parable Stream

To establish Sophia's role in creating the Wisdom language in Proverbs and establishing the metaphors Jesus uses in the New Testament, we will follow the parable stream as they develop in the Old and New Testament. Then, to show the confluence of ideas between the East and the West during Jesus' lifetime, we compare the Biblical parable stream with that of the Upanishads. It seems the Upanishads of India have a very comparable series of parables that end up exactly the same way.

Let the dialog begin. Jesus tells us to seek and find:

> Seek and you will find;
> Knock and the door will be opened."
>
> Matthew 7:7

In Proverbs, we not only seek God, we are to seek Him desperately, to "plea" and "cry" for knowledge of God:

> If your plea is for clear perception,
>
> If you cry out for discernment,
>
> If you look for it as if it were silver,
>
> And seek it as if for buried treasure,
>
> You will understand what fear of Yahweh is,
>
> And discover Knowledge of God.
>
> Proverbs 2:3-5

Buried treasure in Proverbs? We remember Jesus' parable of the buried treasure:

> The Kingdom of Heaven is like treasure buried in a field which someone has found; he hides it again, goes off happy, sells everything he owns and buys the field. Again, the Kingdom of Heaven is like a merchant looking for fine pearls; when he finds one of great value, he goes and sells everything he owns and purchases it.
>
> Matthew 13:44-46

In both Proverbs and Matthew, the "Kingdom of God" (Matthew) and "knowledge of God" (Proverbs) are compared to highly valued treasure, including the pearls of great value. These are metaphors for something that is so valuable that we will give up everything we own in order to have that jewel. Knowledge of the Kingdom of God is so valuable it is worth selling all that we have to find it. In Proverbs, in the Gospels, and in the Upanishads, realizing God's presence is worth more than all these things.

> For Sophia is more precious than pearls,
> And Nothing else is as worthy to desire.
>
> Proverbs 8:11

> Do not store up treasures for yourselves on earth,
> Where moths and woodworms destroy them,
> And thieves can break in and steal.
> But store up treasures for yourselves in the Kingdom of Heaven,
> Where neither moth nor woodworms destroy them,
> And thieves cannot break in and steal.
>
> Jesus: Matthew 6:19-20

> I know that earthly treasure is transient,
> And never can I reach the eternal through them.
> Hence I have renounced all my desires for earthly treasures
> To win the eternal through the guru's instruction.
>
> Katha Upanishads: (30)

So why did Proverbs, Jesus, and the Upanishads use treasure as the goal? They are using treasure as a metaphor for what we want most in life:

> For where your treasure is, there will your heart be also.
>
> Matthew 6:21

> You are what your deep, driving desire is.
> As your desire is, so is your will;
> As your will is, so is your deed;

As your deed is, so is your destiny.

> Forest Upanishad, (31)

Perceiving the world as God's Kingdom should be your greatest treasure, your highest priority in life. That is why we should seek the Kingdom of God first, before anything else.

We might say that what our "deep, driving desire is" is determined emotionally, in our hearts. In this context, the Upanishads take this next step:

> When all the desires that surge in the heart are renounced,
> The mortal becomes immortal.
> When all the knots that strangle the heart
> Are loosened, the mortal becomes immortal,
> Here in this very life.
>
> Forest Upanishad (32)

Not surprisingly, we find agreement in the Wisdom books of the Bible.

> For the fascination of evil throws good things in the shade,
> And the whirlwind of desire corrupts a simple heart.
>
> Wisdom 4:12

So we are held back by our desires for pleasure and material gain rather than seeking and finding God. But the reward is there for those who have a "pure heart."

God can be realized by the pure in heart

> Chandogya Upanishad (33)

The pure of heart? We remember that from the Beatitudes.

Blessed are the pure of heart,
For they shall see God.

> Matthew 5:8 (Beatitudes)

Thus in both the East and West, in the Upanishads and the Gospel, we are to seek and find God, and in both the pure of heart will see God. Isn't that remarkable?

Chapter Eleven: *Proverbs*

The Best Way to Find Sophia Is by Loving Her

So the goal has been set. We are to seek and find the Kingdom of God, God's presence in the world, to become Enlightened. Sophia teaches us how to perceive God as active within us and in the world by changing the way we perceive the world through the use of language: words with mystical meaning, teaching with parables, and sacramental rituals. We yoke our passions, pray and meditate, and practice our spiritual discipline, perhaps for years, perhaps for a lifetime.

> But then in Proverbs, Sophia provides a short cut:
> I love those who love me;
> Those who seek me eagerly shall find Me.
> Proverbs 8:17

Jesus says "seek and you will find." Sophia reflects these same words back to Herself. "Those who seek me eagerly will find Me." And again, these concepts are the same in the Upanishads:

> ... God reveals Himself to the one who longs for the Self.
> Those who long for the Self with all their heart

Are chosen by the Self as His (or Her) own.

> Mundaka Upanishad (34)

Note that in the Upanishads, the Wisdom books of the Old Testament, and the Gospel, God chooses who He/She Enlightens. As Sophia is a Person, it is not surprising that She would want to have Communion with those who love Her.

We should understand that Communion with God is not just for us, for "me." This is something God wants also. Although the search may be daunting, both the yogis of India and the Bible agree that God wants us to be enlightened, and Sophia draws us ever towards Her. The Hindus say that if we take one step towards God, God will take five leaping steps towards us. And don't forget, Jesus said, "Seek and you will find; knock and the door will be opened." Christians need to keep Him to His promise.

Prayer Is an Act of Belief and Devotion

Prayer is perhaps the first act of love or devotion to Sophia. In prayer we address Her as a Person who is real and cares what we think, feel, and say. Mystics of the Bible and of other lands all describe God as "Light," "Love," "Spirit," and a Being, a Person. The image of God as the Holy Spirit is that of Sophia in the Wisdom books. The prayer that begins the book is based on the words of the original, entirely Orthodox Bible.

Belief or what is called faith comes first. We are used to having faith in God the Father, but He is up in heaven. Jesus is too, according to some, but I don't think so. I have friends who see Him around still. When Jesus left He said He'd send the Holy Spirit. The Holy Spirit is the living God who is here with us now. She watches over us, shelters us, feeds us with life and grace, and is like our Mother. Or, if you prefer, She is your forever Bride and Beloved. They are both called Sophia in the Judeo-Christian Wisdom books of the Old and New Testaments.

Meditation is the next step in loving devotion. We noted earlier that philosophers, Neo-Platonists, and early Christians, including St. Augustine, meditated on "the image of God's Goodness" to experience God. Solomon defined Sophia to be the "image of God's Goodness." Meditation on Sophia is confirmed in the book of Ecclesiasticus: "Happy are they who meditate on Sophia."

As encouragement, I offer the following passage that emphasizes Sophia's attractiveness and availability to those who love Her:

> Sophia is bright, and does not grow dim.
> She can readily be seen by those who love Her,
> And found by those who look for Her.
> Quick to anticipate those who desire Her,
> She makes Herself known to them.
> Wisdom 6:12-14

Note that this method of finding Sophia by loving Her parallels the Greatest Commandment: We are to love God with all our hearts, minds and souls. Loving God is not only the goal of the Greatest Commandment, but it is also the mystical method by which we can know God intimately, have Communion with God.

Devotional Music, Singing, and Dancing

Devotional religious music of both the East and West is one of religions greatest and most glorious gifts to mankind from the hearts of composer, singer, and orchestra. As war and killing are on one side of the dialectic, singing God's praises is on the other. I love the classical church music of the West, and of course the Messiah, but that is generally for listening and performed by the organist and a special choir. Join the special choir if you are capable, but many are left in the pews to listen. But what I would like to address is community singing where everyone is involved. I remember when the folk guitar first entered into church services. It was the sixties, and folk was cool and not too loud. There is more group singing in Christian churches now, and now we even have Christian rock. But then the African Americans have been ahead of us all with Gospel and involving all those emotions. I love the Gospel music churches that rock the audience. In India they chant God's name as one voice or in back and forth in sing/response style. The point is, it's easy and repetitive and everyone can sing and as everyone is singing you don't have to have a good voice, you just have to love God. By engaging the heart and singing your love for God it supercharges meditation practice. Singing God's name might make you happier than even meditating faster. But actually, singing God's names is singing meditation. In India it is said that if you have total love for God, *Kevala Bhakti*, you become God. Loving devotion to God is the fastest and easiest way to seek and find Sophia. Bhakti devotion is the rocket ship method of knowing God, and it is a lot of fun making it an "easy" yoga practice.

Chapter Twelve: *The Kingdom of God*

Where Is This Kingdom of God We Are to Seek and Find?

Those of us raised in the Christian tradition remember Jesus' admonition, "Seek first the Kingdom of God." This must be pretty important if Jesus tells us to seek the Kingdom of God first, before we do anything else. "To seek" is a verb; Jesus is telling us to act and act now! However, I know of no Christians in my neighborhood actively seeking the Kingdom of God.

Perhaps nobody is looking because they don't know where to look for this mysterious Kingdom of God. This seems to be a common problem in the Bible. In the New Testament, the scribes, scholars and Pharisees confronted Jesus and asked Him directly, "Where is this Kingdom of God you are always talking about." Perhaps we can determine where this kingdom of God is by Jesus' response. The problem is, there are several translations of Jesus' reply. The first translation comes from the classic King James Bible:

> The kingdom of God is inside of you.
> Luke 17:21

This is a remarkable reply. In the East, this divine Being inside each of us as Consciousness itself is the Self. Jesus refers to this Self in the second part of the Greatest Commandment, "Love your neighbor as your Self." Christians might recognize the Self as the Christ Consciousness inside all of us. However, although more and more Christians recognize Christ Consciousness, neither Jewish nor Christian traditions sponsor the Self as God. It sounds blasphemous, doesn't it? We will explore the concept of the Self later in this book, but let us see if there are different views on where to find the Kingdom of God that work better in the Judeo-Christian tradition.

"The Kingdom of God Is Amongst You"

More recent translations of the Bible, including the *New American Standard* version and my *Jerusalem Bible*, tell us to seek outside of ourselves to find the Kingdom of God. These translations have Jesus responding, "The Kingdom of God is amongst you." The explanation is that Jesus was talking to a group of people rather than just one person, and the Kingdom of God is right there "amongst" them. As "amongst them" would seem to limit the size of the kingdom, we will assume this means that the Kingdom of God is all around and about us.

I have no problem with this translation either. The problem is that when we look around ourselves we see sky and trees and people, but where is that Kingdom of God? As we know the Kingdom of God is a special place, it can't be here, can it? If we are looking for God's presence in the world, we are confronted by His invisibility and transcendence. Although the translation that the Kingdom of God "is amongst us" may have merit, when I actually look about, I really don't see any Kingdom of God anywhere.

One of the other excuses Christians give for not seeking the Kingdom of God is that it is "already here." Jesus died for our sins and now we are in the post-Messianic Age and the gates of heaven are open. But with this logic, we get to the same spot. If it is here, where is it, or what makes this Kingdom of God so special? We are again confronted by the Kingdom of God's invisibility.

The mystery remains.

So we have contradictory translations of where we are to look for "the Kingdom of God," inside or outside ourselves, but both remain invisible. Let us broaden our search for the location of this great kingdom to sources outside the Bible. Perhaps we could obtain needed clarification if we broadened our search for more literary evidence.

The Gospel of St. Thomas

There are two sources that seem to shed light on our problem defining where the Kingdom of God is. The first source, which is somewhat controversial, is from a different translation of Jesus' answer to this same question in the Gospel of Thomas. Thomas' Gospel focuses on Jesus' parables, many of which are the same as in the Synoptic Gospels almost word for word. But the almost is what seems to be wrong as there is often a twist in their meaning, a mysteriously different tone and the wording that doesn't sound like the Jesus of the Synoptic Gospels at all. These changes make Thomas' parables more difficult to understand.

Because the tone of the Gospel of Thomas is different in tone than the Synoptic Gospels, many traditional Christians regard Thomas's Gospel as a "fake" and a "fraud." Others, often of a more liberal, Eastern or mystical persuasion, relish it as the new Fifth Gospel. (35) Hollywood even made a "B grade" movie, *Stigmata* featuring one of the Gospel's more famous passages:

> Turn over a rock,
>
> And I am there...
>
> Gospel of Thomas (36)

That sounds pretty Buddhist, doesn't it? The point here is that Thomas and the producers of the movie thought we didn't need big churches or authorities to show us God. God is everywhere, even under rocks. On the other hand, churches can also be comfortable places to gather in community and worship God. I have no problem worshiping Sophia in cathedrals of rock or of in a forest cathedral of trees. God is omnipresent both places.

In Thomas' version of the parable, it is not the scribes and Pharisees asking Jesus about the Kingdom of God, but His followers, and they do not ask where it is, but when it will come. Jesus responds by telling them exactly where the Kingdom of God is:

> His followers said to Him, "When will the Kingdom come?" Jesus answered, "It will not come by watching for it. It will not be said, "Look, here it is," or "Look, there it is." Rather, the Father's Kingdom is spread out upon the earth, and people do not see it."
>
> Gospel of Thomas (37)

This is a compelling response, is it not? Although many people will not like Jesus' rather direct answer, it does answer the question. "Where is the Kingdom of God?" *It is right there in front of you! You can't see it because you don't perceive it that way; you don't have eyes that see or ears that hear.*

Background on Thomas the Apostle

Thomas the Apostle is nicknamed "the Twin." In the traditional gospels, Thomas asks for physical proof of Jesus' Resurrection, which is taken as a lack of faith. I differ and take Thomas's side. "Show me." If I was Thomas, and they said Jesus was alive, I would want to see Him alive too, wouldn't you? And because Thomas demands evidence, Jesus does appear to Him.

Thomas also appears in the Gospel of Mary Magdalene. (38) There are many versions of the Gospels: final Apocalypses, Acts of different Apostles penned after Jesus ascended into heaven. Of the historical literature about the formulation of the Christian Church, the Gospel of Mary Magdalene stands out, not only because it is Mary Magdalene but also because the scene is quite dramatic. In the gospel, Mary Magdalene confronts St. Peter. Mary wants to take the Wisdom path Jesus had taught, focusing on "seeking and finding" God and spreading the good news. Peter takes a more political approach and tries to establish a more political Jewish sect based on Jesus' communal idealism, which is based on trust. St. Thomas sides with Mary Magdalene when the Apostles split over which direction Christianity should take. We find in Acts of the Apostles St. Peter's Commune doesn't last long, but falls apart due to extensive external and internal struggles. Then the curtain closes on St. Peter in Jerusalem, and the scene turns to St. Paul's ministry. Although Mary Madeline disappears from scripture, she continues on in legend.

In the Acts of Thomas, not to be confused with the Gospel of

Thomas, there is a record of St. Thomas going to India. According to this document, after Jesus left His body, the Apostles "drew lots" to carry the news back in India. It seems there must have been someone in India interested in Jesus' mission. St. Thomas drew the winning "lot," traveled to India, and did extensive missionary work there. In India, they claim Thomas did indeed establish several Christian parishes there, particularly in the Kerala Province. Christian churches in Kerala, India, far away from the Holy Land, are the oldest continuously Christian communities in the world.

The Witness of the Mystics

The second non-Biblical source of evidence I would offer for directions to the Kingdom of God is not as controversial. It is not, however, as authoritative as Jesus or an Apostle. This story comes from a mystic, a Christian saint named Angela of Foligno, who described his experienced of the Kingdom of God here on earth in writing.

> The eyes of my soul were opened, and I beheld the plentitude of God wherein I did comprehend the whole world, both here and beyond the sea, and the abyss and ocean and all things. In all these things I beheld naught save the divine power, in a manner assuredly indescribable; so that through excess of marveling the soul cried with a loud voice, saying, "This whole world is full of God!"
>
> Teachings of Christian Mystics (39)

Wow. "This whole world is full of God." If the world is "full of God," then it must be the "Kingdom of God." We also note Angela's reference to all things being filled with God's "Power." We recognize Sophia is the "Power of God" and omnipotent. In everything, "I beheld naught save the divine Power." "This whole world is full of God" because Sophia the Holy Spirit is God.

In her witness, Angela states she perceived the Kingdom of God through mystical experience. She said, "the eyes of my soul were opened." I expect these are the "eyes" that Jesus talked about when He asked, "Don't you have eyes that can see, ears that can hear?"

Summary of How to Find the Kingdom of God

Given the evidence so far on where to look for the Kingdom of God, I would deduce that the Kingdom of God is all around us, but we don't perceive it that way. We are not look for it some place or some time, it is here about us now. However, we need to make some jump in the way we perceive the world so we realize it really is the Kingdom of God. Sophia teaches us about the Kingdom of God through parables, but there is a short cut to finding this hidden kingdom. According to the Wisdom books of the Bible, we should seek and find Sophia because it is She who shows us that Kingdom.

> Sophia shows the virtuous man the Kingdom of God,
> And teaches him the knowledge of Holy Things.
> Wisdom 10:10

And it seems, according to Angela, recognizing Sophia's presence in all things as the Power of God, the Energy of God, is what the Kingdom of God is. So discover Sophia, and see how it is all God.

Finding the Kingdom of God isn't going to be anything like seeking and finding a lost tool somewhere. It seems we must work at this seeking just as Angela or Solomon did by praying, meditating, receiving the sacraments, learning how to think differently, and most importantly, by loving Sophia. The shortcut is loving devotion to Sophia, and it is very easy to love such a beautiful and wise Holy Spirit of Wisdom.

Chapter Thirteen: *The Upanishads*

Did the "Kingdom of God" Come from the Hindu Upanishads?

Although seeking and finding the Kingdom of God is one of the most important themes in Jesus' ministry and the subject of many of His famous parables, we see little mention of the Kingdom of God in the Old Testament. In fact, in the entire Old Testament, the book of Holy Wisdom is the only place we find the Kingdom of God mentioned. The Protestant and Hebrew Bibles are different from the Catholic and Orthodox Bibles in that they do not contain some of the Wisdom Books, including the Book of Holy Wisdom and Ecclesiasticus. This means that in no place in the Hebrew or Protestant Bible (including the King James Version) do we find any mention of the Kingdom of God in the Old Testament.

Well, this is not entirely true. There is a very closely related "City of God" in Psalms, which is one of the Wisdom books of the Old Testament. Although some of the Psalms are quite old, they were collected and published as a hymnal in Greek in Alexandria, Egypt. The passage referring to the City of God is written in poetic song format to be sung:

> There is a river whose streams refresh the City of God
> And it sanctifies the dwelling of the Most High.

God is inside the city, She can never fall;

Psalms 46:4-5

So God is present in the City of God. That is what makes it the City of God. This city is the dwelling place of God. The psalm continues:

All over the world He puts an end to wars,

He breaks the bow, He snaps the spear,

He gives shields to the flames,

Be silent and know I am God.

Psalms 46:9-10

The last line is a favorite of those who understand that the Wisdom writers of the Bible meditated. In some forms of meditation, for example following the breath, the objective is to silence the mind. It is in the silence of meditation that we can "hear the unheard." The objective of this silence is knowledge of God or Enlightenment, to "know I Am God." Isn't it interesting that Enlightenment, intimate Knowledge of God, is paired with putting an end to wars in this passage? There is no war in the City of God. The City of God theme is then reflected in the New Testament at the end of Revelations:

Then the angel showed me the River of Life,

Rising from the throne of God and of the Lamb,

And flowing crystal-clear down the middle of the city street.

On either side of the river were the trees of life...

Revelations 22:1-2,17

What beautiful, metaphorical poetry. The City of God is alive with imagery of water as a metaphor for Spirit, like the story of the Samaritan woman at the well who Jesus offers "Living Water" feeding the trees of life (perhaps our nervous system).

> Anyone who drinks the water that I shall give
> Will never by thirsty again:
> The water that I shall give
> Will turn into a spring inside him,
> Welling up to Eternal Life.
>
> John 4:13-14,22

Living Water from a spring inside of us welling up to Eternal Life! Don't we all thirst for this water? And remember Sophia gives the waters of Eternal Life "for free" in Revelations.

The poetry of the Wisdom Literature throughout the Bible provides us with a tapestry of metaphors linking water to Spirit. We find springs and fountains, streams and rivers flowing with the pure, "crystal clear water" of Eternal Life into the City of God. It is like a new Garden of Eden, a new paradise. But to find it we need the Holy Spirit of Wisdom and Perception, Sophia, to show it to us.

The "Kingdom of God" Is Described Often in the Upanishads

Although we rarely find mention of the Kingdom of God in the Old Testament, we find numerous references to the "Kingdom of God," the "City of God," the "Realm of God," "the World of Brahman," and "the

Kingdom of Heaven on earth" in the Upanishads. Could we find out more about what Jesus meant by saying we should seek the Kingdom of God first by researching the Upanishads?

The Upanishads

The Upanishads are dialogs between an Enlightened Master and a student. The Upanishads lay out the Hindu view of God and the cosmos, and how humans find Enlightenment. The oldest Upanishads were added onto the even more ancient Vedas. The best guess for dating the classic Upanishads is 600-300 BCE, but that may have been when Western historians became aware of them as we remember that the Great Library of Alexandria was founded in about 300 BCE. Although there are also modern Upanishads written after Jesus was born, the classic Upanishads quoted here were in existence before the Wisdom books of the Bible were written. I expect the writers of the Wisdom books knew of them because they were included in the collections of the library by say 100 BCE when the late Wisdom books were being written and would have been available in Alexandria for study by young Rabbinical students during Jesus' formative years.

Here is a discussion of the Kingdom of God from the Chandogya Upanishad:

> The Self is hidden in the Lotus of the Heart.
> Those who see themselves in all creatures
> Go day by day into the World of Brahman [God]
> Hidden in the heart.
>
> Established in peace, they rise above body consciousness

> To the supreme light of the Self.
> Immortal, free from fear, this Self is Brahman, called the Truth.
> Only those who are pure and self-controlled
> Can find this World of Brahman.
> In that world, in all the worlds,
> They live in perfect freedom.
>
> Chandogya Upanishad (40)

This is a fairly complete summary description of the Kingdom of God, here called the World of Brahman/God, from a Hindu perspective. God is found in mystical experience inside yourself, residing inside our hearts, inside our own consciousness. In this state of perception, we rise above body consciousness to experience "the supreme Light of the Self," which I expect is the same as the "Eternal Light," as a Person, Sophia. We then rise to "Truth" and to "perfect freedom." This is very similar to Jesus' words in St. John's Gospel:

> If you make my word your home
> You will indeed be my disciples,
> You will learn the truth,
> And the truth shall make you free.
>
> John 8:31-32

Of special note in the Chandogya passage is that we perceive everything to be One in God in this state: "Where there is unity, One without a second. That is the World of Brahman (God)." The experience of the Oneness of all things in God is a common theme to all mystical literature. Here we remember Plotinus, the Neo-Platonist, who inspired St. Augustine to seek God by meditating "on the image of God's Goodness." The name of Plotinus's book is *Towards the One*. The Upanishads tell us what the change in perception we must undergo entails. We see all things as One. We see our Selves in all creatures, see them as members of Christ's Mystical Body.

In the Chandogya Upanishad, obtaining the Kingdom of God is the "supreme goal of life":

> Where there is unity, one without a second,
> That is the World of Brahman (Kingdom of God).
> This is the supreme goal of life,
> The supreme treasure, the supreme joy.
> Those who do not seek this supreme goal
> Live on but a fraction of this joy.
>
> Forest Upanishad (41)

In the Upanishads, finding the Kingdom of God is the supreme goal in life, "the supreme treasure, the supreme joy." Who doesn't want to live in God's Kingdom of joy? This Upanishad motivates us to do what Jesus tells us to do: "Seek first the Kingdom of God" and you will find the Eternal Life, the Eternal Light, and limitless joy. Before discovering this Kingdom, we live on a fraction of the joy.

In both the Upanishads and the gospel, the Kingdom of God fulfills all our needs:

> Seek first the Kingdom of God, and His righteousness and
> all these other things will be given to you as well.
>
> Matthew 6:33

> In the City of Brahman [God] is a secret dwelling,
> The lotus of the heart.
> Within this dwelling is a space,
> And within that space is the fulfillment of our desires,
> What is within that space should be longed for and realized.
>
> Chandogya Upanishad (42)

In the Upanishads and the gospel all our needs are fulfilled, our desires quieted, and we are filled with joy at being in the Kingdom of God. There we find peace, and we become instruments to spread that peace:

> May we hear only what is good for all.
> May we see only what is good for all.
> May we serve you, Lord of Love, all our lives.
> May we be used to spread Your peace on earth.
>
> The Breath of Life/Prashna Upanishad (43)

The Lord of Love's peace here in Hindu scripture is the same as "Peace of the Lord" in Christianity. It is a part of the Wisdom vocabulary, especially in John. We hug people in our services and with them we say, "May the peace of the Lord be with you." It is from this position of inner peace that we are able to bring "peace on earth." It is called peace on earth because we don't have to war anymore. All our needs and desires are fulfilled; we appreciate the bounty and plentitude of God's creation; we are grateful for the joy of Being:

> All this is full. All that is full.
>
> From fullness comes fullness,
>
> When fullness is taken from fullness,
>
> And fullness still remains.
>
> Om shanti, shanti, shanti
>
> Isha Upanishad (44)

Is it not interesting how many Christian themes, concepts, and metaphors are similar in both the Upanishads and the Wisdom Literature of the Bible? In the Upanishads and the Wisdom Literature, not only are both Kingdoms of God similar, but so is the style in which they are written. I fully expect the writers of the Septuagint Bible met the Upanishads at the great Library of Alexandria, Egypt.

Chapter Fourteen: *The Council of Nicaea*

Emperor Constantine Rejects Sophia and Institutionalizes Imperial Roman Law and Conquests

The Council of Nicaea (325 AD) unified and institutionalized the theologically diverse, nascent Christian Church under the authority of the Roman Emperor Constantine. We don't hear much about it, but Roman emperors managed and conducted the first seven Ecumenical Councils before the Bishop of Rome assumed the role of Pope. The emperor was the "Pontiff" of all the legal, Pagan religions within the Roman Empire, so that when he legalized Christianity, it came under his jurisdiction. The emperor was infallible because he was the final decider with the Roman legions and the imperial purse strings to back him up. At the Nicene Council, the Roman Christian Church established the primary tenants of Christianity, which were summarized in the Nicene Creed. This became dogmatic truth all Christians had to believe in to be members of the universal, institutional Church of the Roman Empire, the Roman Catholic Church. Faith in Jesus meant belief in church dogma and obedience to the Pontiff, the Roman Emperor Constantine.

The Nicene Council established Jesus as the "Word of God," the second Person of the Trinity, and thus divine, which won universal approval and the Roman Emperor Constantine sainthood. To make way for Jesus as the Word of God, Constantine jettisoned Sophia not only as the Word of God but also as a divine Person or Being so She could not be the Holy Spirit.

The debate over Sophia's divinity was one of the highlights of the Council of Nicaea. The winner, Athanasius, is a saint in the Roman Church. Arius, the loser, became perhaps the most famous heretic of all time for arguing that Jesus was not God, an argument he never made. The problem was more defining our relationship with God, and the emperor didn't want the Holy Spirit having Communion with people and Enlightening them. Establish Jesus as the Word, jettison Sophia, and the people would focus on being useful and advance themselves by advancing the interests of the Roman Empire rather than seeking the invisible, hearing the unheard. What use are a bunch of monks when you need consumers, slaves, laborers, merchants, and soldiers to conquer or prevent your country from being conquered. And if everyone is connected to God so whatever you do to the least of your slaves or criminals you do to Jesus Christ, how could you maintain order without crucifying criminals and other trash?

It was a setup debate, with Athanasius representing the emperor's side and the emperor making the final decision. Arius was a charismatic leader, who made waves amongst the people for making Jesus more human-thinking. This would make human beings more important to the Emperor. As his writings and arguments were banned and burned, we know little about what he really thought. Instead, we hear the accusations against him.

The lines indicating Sophia was or was not divine had long been debated for decades within the Church. The key question broke down to, does God create "Holy Wisdom," or does He "possess" Holy Wisdom? To show Sophia was not divine, Athanasius first quoted Proverbs where it says that Sophia was the "first creation" of God, then he added, "Jesus was begotten, not made." This is a reflection of the monotheistic model of God where God is our perfect, transcendent creator while we and the world are created and imperfect. The logic was, as Sophia was created, She cannot be divine. Jesus was instead "begotten," whatever that means.

Should We Blame the Poet for His Bad Choice of Words?

It says in the Wisdom books of the Bible that Sophia is divine, "the Breath of God," "the Word of God," "the Holy Spirit of God." But how can She be God if She was "created?" I want to pause and note the irony of this statement. Aren't "the Breath of God" and "the Word of God" created by God? Is "the Word of God" divine? How about the Holy Spirit?

One is tempted to blame the poet who wrote Proverbs for choosing the word "created" to describe Sophia. *The writer of Proverbs should have known Sophia was divine. Why did that dumb writer use the term "created?" Doesn't he know that you can't be God if you are created?* From this, one could deduce that perhaps the writer should have Sophia saying, "God emanated me" or better yet, "God begot me." Perhaps the writer of Wisdom and the New Testament just had a better vocabulary. There, the Holy Spirit seems to have better verbs for describing how the Holy Spirit comes out of both Jesus and God.

But then one could argue that "create" is not all that bad a word, really. "Create" is one of those words that has a lot of meanings. Isn't the word "create" pretty close to "emanate," and doesn't it sound better? Is not the Word of God created in God's mind and spoken? Is not speaking an act of creation?

Others, including St. Jerome, concluded that God "possessed" Holy Wisdom. Now that makes sense. God wasn't dumb or a void. Certainly, God possesses Holy Wisdom. I would push the concept even further and say God is Holy Wisdom – God is wise. Holy Wisdom then emanated from God as his "power" and "glory" and is active in the world. Or, Holy Wisdom is the Power and the Glory of God being the universe. Note again that Constantine used the monotheistic model of God rather than the universe as God Being.

The Sun and Sunlight Metaphor for God

The sun has served as a metaphor for God in many religions because the sun creates light, which gives the planet warmth, light, thus giving the planet life. In this metaphorical model, the sun becomes God the Father, the Creator, and the light of the Creator sun, "the power and glory of God," or Sophia. We do not see the sun; we see the sun's glory and light, we see the "energy of God," who is Sophia. Actually, this model for God, which allows for Sophia to be created, exists in India, and it works for me.

It is also possible that the writer of Proverbs and the writer of Wisdom had different ideas of who Sophia really was. Proverbs was written earlier, and perhaps recognition of Sophia's divinity came later. She certainly is divine in the book of Holy Wisdom, and I think She is wonderful in Proverbs. Just ignore the word "create" and see how She pleases God and plays with the Sons of Man.

Bottom line, I think Constantine and Athanasius were making too much of a single word with too many meanings to get rid of Sophia. Athanasius got away with it by promoting Jesus as God and a champion of the people. We don't mind Jesus being divine, but I don't think he was justified in jettisoning Sophia, and even with Jesus as the Son, the second Person of the Trinity, there was still a spot open of the Holy Spirit where they could have installed Her where She should be. This was a very bad decision had a huge impact on Christianity.

What Did the Emperor Gain?

I would define the primary achievements of Constantine at Nicaea and in the forthcoming institutionalization of the Church as the following:

- Established Jesus as the Word of God, the second Person of the Trinity and thus divine.
- Determined Sophia was not divine but a made up character used as a metaphor, who tells us how wise Jewish historical figures were.
- Established the Nicene Creed (in its incomplete form) as the essential dogma all Christians must believe in order to be Christians.
- Determined which books in the Bible were canonical, "the Word of God," and thus legally binding documents representing God's will on earth.
- Adopted the one life/heaven or hell model for what happens after death over reincarnation.

At Nicaea, the Word of God became a document, a legal book that purports to express what God wants. This is far different from the Word of God being a Person, like Jesus or Sophia, for that matter. In a sense, Jesus and Sophia as existent Persons doesn't matter because we have the

"Word of God" captured in print. The law of the land as described in the Pentateuch, the law of Ptolemaic Egypt, was adapted by the Roman Empire and institutionalized into the Law of the Orthodox Roman Catholic Church and Western Christian governments of that time.

The Pentateuch Contains Great Stories

Before I take on the Pentateuch, I must say what is good about it. The first five books of the best-selling book of all time, the Bible, is regarded by billions of people to be "the Word of God and correct in every detail," if interpreted properly. Without a doubt, the Pentateuch was the most successful nation-building literary exercises ever. Common belief in these stories and history has inspired Christian nations to identify with the chosen people of God and their law, history, and values for centuries. There are wonderful stories. Who can forget the contest where the underdog, David, defeats the giant Goliath in mortal combat using advanced technology – the sling and rock over the sword and shield – to win for God's side. There are stories of great warrior heroes, almost superhero saints, sent by God to defeat Israel's evil enemies.

My favorite Biblical story as a kid was about Sampson, the strong man who lost his hair and strength to the seductress Delilah, a secret agent of the enemy. Weak and blind, Sampson was forced to labor for the enemy. He got his revenge on his enemies when he grew his hair back and brought down the Pagan temple on his himself and his oppressors.

There are also important religious themes in the Pentateuch which have inspired minorities, like the Jewish people's escape from captivity. African American communities have celebrated the Jews escaping their enslavement since before the Civil War. In fact, this is a universal theme we can all identify with. Don't we all want to be the chosen people of God? Don't we all want to be politically free and identify with the children of God?

We are still very invested in war superhero stories today. Isn't Sampson's plight much like that of Conan the Barbarian or other comic books? But this is not heavy theology, and it really isn't religion. This is superhero stuff for us to admire and wish we were like them, people to model after. When you think about it, the stories in the Pentateuch aren't very religious at all. There is little talk in the Pentateuch about human beings having souls or what happens after we die or how we, the little people, can relate to God until we get to the Prophets and Wisdom books of the Bible.

The Legal Books of the Pentateuch Institutionalized Imperial Society

Please understand that I am not against all the laws in the legal books of the Pentateuch. I think it is a good idea to follow the Ten Commandments, and the Golden Rule has Old Testament origins. Follow those laws and do what Jesus says to do first. My problem with the Pentateuch is not the stories and histories. My problem is with the laws in the Legal books of the Pentateuch that structure people's relationship with each other, with the imperial economy, and with God.

The easiest example of "bad" Pentateuch law is slavery. Slavery was not only permitted in the Bible but regulated. It was built into the economy. Essentially you went into slavery if you couldn't pay your debts. The regulation included how the owner could punish the slave for not doing his will. According to Old Testament law, the slave holder could beat their slave to death if they did not die right away. If they linger for three days before dying, it is OK. If he or she dies right away, you had to pay the penalty with a sacrifice made at the temple. After all, the slave was the property of the owner. Now imagine sex slavery, which was also common. Rather than become a slave, you could offer your daughter to be an additional wife of the debt holder if she was ripe. This is how woman became "property" in imperial society. Women were also the booty of war. The classic Homeric epic *The Iliad* begins with Achilles and the King arguing over who gets the most beautiful woman in the city they just conquered.

The Slave as "the Least of Us"

If you wanted the definition of "the least of us" (reference to Matthew 25: "Whatever you do to the least of us, you do unto me.") one example would be the slave in Roman society, perchance the gladiator. The gladiators were slaves bred like dogs to fight one another for entertainment. Is not the defeated gladiator, wounded and bleeding, awaiting the decision of the emperor whether he gets a "thumb up" or "thumb down," one of the least of us?

But slavery doesn't just dehumanize the slave, it dehumanizes everyone in society. All the people of Rome cheered the winning gladiator and enjoyed seeing the weak get killed and the Christians eaten by lions. That was justice in action. That was entertainment. And why do we, the popular chorus of today, so enjoy the fight of today's gladiators as they pummel each other into unconsciousness in boxing or mixed martial arts? Why is our will to win so strong we get into a ring or a fight or war voluntarily just so we can show we're tougher and meaner?

I hope the reader can see how attractive Christianity was to the slave, who actually had an ally in Jesus Christ who loved them and fed them and who died so they could be free. In Christianity, the common man was changed from a real nobody to a "Child of God."

Cruel Punishments

We would note that many of the criminal sentences for capital crimes in the Pentateuch, of which there were many, amounted to torturing the prisoner to death. The Romans standard method of capital punishment was crucifixion, also making the criminals parting from life as painful as possible as an example to other low-lifes. The Old Testament legal books provide similarly torturous punishments for acts of sexual perversion, which seems odd. What we call manslaughter, killings in bar fights, was lawful in some towns frequented by mercenaries and imperial warriors. The continuance of torturous practices throughout Europe, especially in Great Britain, disgusted the Founding Fathers of our country who recognized and prohibited "cruel and unusual" punishments and testifying against yourself in the Bill of Rights.

The Midian War

Another moral hurdle for the Pentateuch is the justification of imperial wars, including the Midian War described in the book of Numbers. For those who have not read the Old Testament for themselves, this passage might be a shocker. However, it is well known by the opponents of Christianity. From writers on the Left side of the aisle, in both bookstores and on the Internet, you hear a lot of blame put on Christianity for this war. But that is exactly the opposite of how I regard it. My point is this isn't Christianity at all. This is the exact opposite of Jesus' Way. In this story from Numbers, God does not "abhor" war. God demands war and genocide, sacrifices and holocausts, because he is a jealous God.

The background of the story is that a group of women from a competing religion seduced Jewish warriors into worshiping their god. So now God is very jealous and wants vengeance.

> Moses put his armies in the field, one thousand from each tribe: Moses put them to the field with Phinehas, the son of Eleazar the priest, to go with them carrying the sacred vessels and the trumpets for sounding the alarm.
>
> ...
>
> They waged the campaign against Midian, as Yahweh had ordered Moses, and they put every male to death. And further, they killed the kings.... They put Balaam to the sword.... The sons of Israel took the Midian women captive with their young children, and plundered all their cattle, all their flocks and all their goods.
>
> ...
>
> Moses was enraged with the commanders of the army. "Why have you spared the lives of the women? These are the very ones who, on Balaam's advice, perverted the sons of Israel and made them renounce Yahweh. So kill all the male children. Kill also all the women who have slept with a man. Spare the lives only of the young girls who have not slept with a man, and take them for your selves.
>
> Numbers 31:7-19

As the story is stated directly in declarative sentences as history in a legal book of the Bible, it seems appropriate to treat it literally. It does not deal with metaphor, but legal standards for breaking "God's law." This is a description of a genocidal war, a holocaust. Moses' army sacrifices men and women alike, takes everything of value, including their land and livestock, and the young virgin girls as sex slaves to appease their god's anger.

The God of the Pentateuch is a Jealous God

Again, as in the case with slavery, because it says in the Bible that God is a jealous god, people believe it. This is not some speculation on my part, but it was built into the Old Testament Ptolemaic concept of God. It is also built into the first of the Ten Commandments. "I am thy Lord thy God. Thou shall have no strange gods before me."

This concept of a jealous god continued through Christian Church history, played a role in the Crusades, and was taken by the West into Colonial times. Here is Francis Bacon (1561-1626), the famous British philosopher (note the deterioration of philosophy by this time) during the early hay day of British Colonialism.

> But the true God hath this attribute, that he is a jealous God; and therefore his worship and religion will endure no mixture nor partner.
>
> Francis Bacon (43)

Thus, Bacon explains the natural antagonism of Western religion and society towards other religions and races. Their God is the only God and He will endure "no mixture nor partner." Note that Francis Bacon lived during the period in which the British colonized the continents of North America, Asia, and Australia and made for themselves an empire on which the sun never set at the expense of the native populations of those lands.

No Invasion of the Holy Land

While studying Old Testament history, I was surprised to read most scholars do not believe there was an invasion of the Holy Land by the twelve tribe of Israel as depicted in the Bible. Some scholars argue that Moses never existed. The Biblical story of the people of God coming out of Egypt and taking the Holy Land through a series of wars is simply wrong. This conclusion is based on solid archeological evidence from the ancient libraries of the Assyrians, rulers of the entire region at the time the Jewish conquest of the Holy Land was to have occurred. Although they kept copious records of everything, they recorded no such invasion of their land and territory. The historical facts do not fit the legend. Essentially, the Old Testament Pentateuch may be a collection of old war stories of composite characters collected and dramatized to create an imperial national identity for the people living under Ptolemaic rule.

According to commonly available sources today (including Wikipedia), everyone was living hospitably in the Holy Land until some nationalists came along and invigorated a once-peaceful nation with illusions of Alexandrian grandeur and imperial wealth based on spreading their superior culture and "God."

The Pentateuch Is on the Wrong Side of Hosea's Dialectic

I hope the idea of God wanting war and genocide is shocking. If our definition of spiritual transformation is our spiritual repulsion to war, this passage is counter transformational. The "god" described in this passage is not the God of Jesus Christ, nor is this god divine Love or Light. This god is some fratricidal Ptolemaic ruler's wet dream of authority and control. I don't know who wrote that particular passage, but I imagine the evil Ptolemy IV writing it and insisting it go into his

Bible as he was paying for it, although it could have been others. It seems most were psychopaths. I feel this story is a real blasphemy against God. It certainly has nothing to do with Jesus' Christianity.

Gnosis in the Pentateuch

Gnosis is mentioned in the Pentateuch but not positively as in the Prophetic, Wisdom, and New Testament books. In an earlier story, Balaam "saw" God and fell on his knees in humility. We like him initially. But this is the same Balaam who was ruler of Midian, who was murdered and his nation sacked in the war as demanded by God. The Tree of Knowledge in Genesis comes very close to being the "Tree of Gnosis," and even the word "Gnosis," which is Enlightenment, is blemished by labeling Gnosticism as a heresy. One of the arguments against the Gnostics was they thought there was a good and bad God. I don't think there is a good and bad God. The Bible was written by human beings, some of whom were inspired by God and others who were inspired by their own vanity, inflated egos, and meanness.

Let us look at the situation from the perspective of Hosea's dialectic. He divides our actions as to what God wants and what God doesn't want, thus separating good and evil. God wants compassion and Communion with God or Enlightenment. God doesn't want wars and genocides. On this divide both the Ptolemaic and Roman Empire are on the "Dark Side." Both were for terrible punishment, even burning in hell for all eternity for some, and total authority for the rulers. There was no compassion or possible Communion with God. Thus, the history of the West has been filled with a history marked by who won which war and who burned up what heretics or witches, or who invaded, colonized, and killed or enslaved what natives of what continent. This is not what God or Jesus or Sophia wanted for us, but the history we got from Emperor Constantine.

In the Prophets, the Wisdom books, and the New Testament, the Sophia and Jesus Wisdom Movement was transformational. They testify to the necessary spiritual reaction against wars and holocausts. They show us the way to be compassionate and how to have intimate Knowledge of God and to be Baptized in the Holy Spirit.

The Dialectic Remained Unresolved After Nicaea

The reaction against Constantine's dictates at Nicaea started almost immediately. First, I should mention that the Roman Catholic Church did not become the one and only institutional church of the empire until two emperors later – under Emperor Theodosius in 380 CE. It is notable that Emperor Constantine was not baptized when he took over the Christian Church but was baptized on his death bed by an Arian priest. The issue of who or what the Holy Spirit is was left undefined at Nicaea. The draft document says only, "and we believe in the Holy Spirit." We will see in a later chapter how St. Basil the Great saved the Holy Spirit and Enlightenment but made the Holy Spirit male and without Sophia's attractive personality. In taking away Sophia, the Emperor also jettisoned God as Mother, a role we remember Sophia played in the New Testament. The ever pure, born without original sin, ever Virgin Mary became Mother of God and thus our almost divine Mother. The metaphorical logic goes that if Mary is Christ's mother, and Christ has a mystical body in which we are all members, thus Mary is our spiritual mother, except, of course, she isn't divine, but She is human.

There was a great deal of worship of the Virgin Mary in the Catholic Church of my youth. I remember looking in at all the old woman staying after mass to say their rosaries in the candlelight and wondering. *What good is that?* The rosary has long been associated with Mother Mary as an instrument of prayer and meditation. My sad and mother took up saying the rosary nightly, and I'd say it with them. It works for me, at least for the glorious mysteries.

The Political Evolution of Our Species After Nicaea

The United States banned institutional slavery during the Civil War, but it has occurred in other countries and in other forms since time began, and of course. there are many kinds of slavery and means of coercing people to do what the money wants. Awakening spirituality played a key role in our society's emancipation from slavery. Perhaps the best evidence is the "Amazing Grace" in which a Scottish ex-slave trader sees the Light, which I expect he actually did. The Quakers and other religions that meditated and read more of the New Testament than the Old also played key roles in freeing the species from institutionalized slavery. This emancipation was opposed by Southerner politicians, who appealed to the slavery regulating laws of the Pentateuch, which they regarded as the natural order and thus the way it should be.

On the issue of war and peace, we have not made as much progress. Although we love our neighbors, promote kindness, don't want to hurt anybody, and hug each other in church, we are once again in a period of continuous wars and mayhem of our own making, building up to the big one. What's the problem?

If you are going to rule in the world, decide which direction history will take, seize the day, you are going to have to live a very worldly life based on advancement, winning, power, friends in high place, and a big, resilient ego. There is a point at which to have your way in the world, it will be necessary to kill because of the importance of the security of the country you represent. If you are running the world and managing such important things, what time is there to seek and find the Kingdom of God, to love God, or regard your neighbor as your Self?

Or perhaps God is simply irrelevant to those under the stress of having to manage money, the wealth of the world, military alliances, and corporate profits, and their debts. Of course, you need a big ego, drive, and a willingness to fight for your clientele. That's what we vote them in for, to fight for us in the halls of Congress, isn't it?

We remember the magazine cover on *Time* magazine indicating God was dead. Perhaps God is not dead to our imperial rulers but irrelevant. And I am not talking about the God that sets rules and laws that we must obey, as those laws are made for and by humans and should be for our benefit. I am talking about a God who loves us and wants us to be happy, to share with each other, as we are His/Her children.

The mystical St. Paul had a solution for the divisions and divisiveness in the Roman society of that time. He "had great hope" in his vision that we are all members of Christ's Mystical Body and thus not divided by race, caste, or Pagan versus Jew but are One. As we do not really understand the Mystical Body of Christ, which is invisible to the worldly, we ignore it and act like animals instead of spiritual Beings. But this is the basis of Christian morality. We are all members of the Mystical Body of Christ such that whatever we do to the least of our brothers, we do to Jesus Christ as Christ Consciousness. This Oneness in God's body implies wars and divisiveness are destructive, and we are meant to act spiritually towards one another. We note that they have no "fear of God," which scripture says is the beginning of Wisdom. Scripture also cautions, "As you sow, so shall you reap." And I think of the trillions of dollars we spend on weapons to kill each other and wonder, "Are these the seeds we sow?"

So we toil at war for millennia and throw away the solution to our instinct to war, who is Sophia, the Holy Spirit of Wisdom. There is a line in the Gospels that blasphemy towards the Holy Spirit is the unpardonable sin. Wow, a sin that God will not forgive? The explanation they generally give is that if you insult the Holy Spirit, She won't be there for you when you need Her. Then I wondered, did Emperor Constantine's rejection of Sophia take Her and our Communion with God away? If Sophia is a just a made-up character, who is going to show us the Kingdom of God, Christ's Mystical Body in which we are all members? If we allow Sophia and Jesus show us the Way, the Truth, and the Life, why kill each other for the glory of Rome?

Chapter Fifteen: *New Testament Wisdom*

Jesus and the Evangelists Affirm Sophia Is the Holy Spirit and the Bride

In the wake of the Imperial edict saying Sophia is not divine, what better way to re-affirm Sophia's position in the Trinity as the Holy Spirit of Wisdom than to quote Jesus, St. John, St. Paul, and the other Evangelists who wrote the New Testament, that the emperor was corrupt, and that through his involvement, he corrupted the Church?

Jesus was God incarnate, the Christ, "the anointed one" of the transformational Wisdom Movement. Jesus opened the Wisdom channels to Spirit, the doors and windows to let in the Light. He gave us access the Holy Spirit of God so that we could gain "full" and "intimate" knowledge of God and find out for ourselves that God is all Good, God is Great, and God loves us and want Communion with us. Through Christ's intercession in our history and His transmission of how we best behave, Jesus was Sophia partner in spreading the Wisdom Movement in the West, which became the Jesus movement in the Holy Land, and ultimately Christianity in all its commercial and spiritual forms.

The Wisdom of the "Greatest Commandment"

As this is going to be a summary chapter of sorts, I wanted to start with the most important contributions of the Wisdom Movement. We begin by focusing on what Jesus tells us to do first: "First seek the Kingdom of God." Hopefully, you now know something about where to look, or who to look for in order to find the Kingdom of God. Sophia shows us God's Kingdom as She is the Power, Glory, and Energy of God active as the universe.

Jesus also placed great importance on "The Greatest Commandment." The first part of the Greatest Commandment is to "love God." This comes naturally as we get to know God because God is Love, Light, and the source of Life and Being. It is also the means by which we find Sophia and experience Her fullness. Loving God is expressed in prayer, meditation, and devotion, for example expressing our love of God by singing. The Wisdom books of the Bible say that God is active in the world as the Word and the Holy Spirit of God and they are both very real and available for a relationship. They are two Persons, but they are One. From what I can tell, the Holy Spirit seems to come out of the Christ, although She can come independently as in Baptism or Confirmation, or Holy Order and marriage in the Wisdom Tradition. The Holy Spirits of both Sophia and Jesus are still alive and active in the world. I have seen and heard much testimony concerning this fact.

Understanding the second part of the Greatest Commandment, "love your neighbor as your Self," is unique to the mystically based religions that recognize God Consciousness is within each person, even though we don't see it even though we don't know it. We are just ignorant, so we act like the animals that we are rather than evolve spiritually into what we can be.

Since the "Self" is a concept that most Westerners do not understand, I would like to explore this concept.

The Self

We discussed how Sophia seeks to change our perception of the world by changing the language we use. "The Self" is a good example. Suddenly, when capitalized, "the Self" means God within each of us as Christ Consciousness. This is a key Wisdom concept, and it comes from the East, the Hindu Yogis through Pythagoras and the philosophers, the lovers of Sophia. In India the Self is God or the Christ Consciousness within each person; in Buddhism it is the Big Buddha. We remember the extensive trade in merchandise and ideas between India and Egypt. Jesus would have known about the Self as it was a part of the Wisdom based theology of that time.

This Self has long been recognized in the East in their sacred literature. The Isha Upanishad, honored as one of the most important Upanishads, tells us a great deal about the Self:

> The Self is everywhere.
> Bright is the Self,
> One, untouched by sin, wise,
> Immanent and transcendent.
> It is He who holds the Universe together.
>
> Isha Upanishad (45)

We might notice some similarities to Sophia. Sophia permeates all things and is omnipresent, like the Self. She is the Eternal Light that outshines the sun, thus quite "bright." Sophia is ever pure, untouched by sin just like the Self. As the Word of God (before Jesus was born), Sophia orders the universe, or we could say She "holds the universe together." In this poem, the Self is God and remarkably similar to Sophia:

Then the mystical discovery of who God is defined:
That very Self Am I.

Isha Upanishad (46)

In the East, as the Self is pure and holy, we are by our natures pure and holy, full of compassion and love. The problem is, we are ignorant of our true natures and identify with the animal side of ourselves. We are selfish in our outlook towards life, and we are hard wired to want, to possess, and to win. But this way is bent on frustration. The goal of life is not wealth, power, authority, and toys. The idea is to evolve into our true selves, our true natures, which we find in Communion with Sophia and the formation of a lasting relationship with God.

Explaining the Self

This presents a problem of how to explain that God is inside us, but we don't know it. The Upanishads explain:

> The Self-existent Lord pierced the senses,
> To turn outward, Thus we look to the world
> Without and see not the Self within us.

Katha Upanishad (47)

The Self doesn't speak but listens, hears but has no ears, doesn't move but is everywhere, doesn't act but participates in all activity, is invisible to the five senses but is the source of their Life and being. The Self is omniscient Consciousness itself, and it sees all we see and feel.

I have heard that many have discovered this Self within. But for others, Sophia seemingly pours in from outside the ego until the mind is filled with Sophia. Either way, Sophia seems to have the same qualities, and it all happens in the mind, in our consciousness, which is inside us anyway, isn't it?

There is "union Communion" with God. In Latin "comm" means "of" and "union" means "union." There is realization of the Self, a sharing of spiritual energy and expansion of consciousness. There is also a shrinking of importance of the little "me," that we think we are. The "me" that I identify with as my animal body is quite imperfect, but it is the best and only tool I have to seek God's presence in the world and love God, and to try and do some good in the world.

The Mystical Body of Christ

The Self, or the Christ Consciousness, within each is key in understanding St. Paul's concept of the Mystical Body of Christ. Now, I understand many liberals don't like St. Paul, but there was more than one writer we call St. Paul. I expect the Epistles of St. Paul are a collection of sermons and letters from the Christian tradition led by St. Paul, included sermons and letters from others. Some Epistles, like St. Paul's Epistle to the Romans, which is quite lengthy, are probably edited compilations of several letters or sermons dealing with specific issues. The St. Paul that I'm addressing is the mystical St. Paul who wrote the Epistle to the Ephesians. Ephesus was a colony of Greece in Turkey. In this Epistle, St. Paul introduces the concept of the "Mystical Body of Christ":

> Jesus is the Head of the Church, which is His Body, which is the manifestation of the fullness of Him who fills all creation.
>
> Ephesians 1:23

We are all members of that body.

> Now we together are Christ's Body.
> 1 Cor. 12:23

The intent is to unite us, realize our union with Christ, that we are all a part of Christ's Mystical body.

> Jesus Christ is the peace between us and has made the two into one and broken down the barriers that divided them, actually destroying in His own Person the hostility to the rules and decrees of law. In Him, both of us, in one Spirit, have come to the Father.
> Ephesians 2:14-15

St. Paul speaks to the "one Spirit" who unites us all in Christ's Body.

> Just as a human body, though it is made of many parts, is a single unit because all these parts, though many, make one body. So it is with Christ. In one Spirit we were baptized, Jews as well as Greeks, slaves as well as citizens, and one Spirit was given us all to drink.
> 1 Cor. 12:12-13

There is one Body of Christ, one Spirit, just as you were all called in one and the same hope. There is one Lord, one faith, one baptism, and one God who is Father of all, over all, through all, and within all.

> Ephesians 4:4-6

What St. Paul seems to be saying is one Body and One Spirit are the same, One God. It is interesting how the St. Paul of the Ephesians tells us how to get to this exalted state.

> Out of His infinite glory may God give you the power, through His Holy Spirit for your hidden Self to grow strong, so that Christ may live in your hearts through faith, then planted in love and built on love will have the strength to understand, until knowing the love of Christ, which is beyond all knowledge, you are filled with the utter fullness of God.
>
> Ephesians 3:16-19

As in India, finding God is likened to awakening and seeing the world for what it is. St. Paul uses the same theme – wake up!

> Wake up from you sleep,
> Rise from the dead,
> And Christ will shine on you.
>
> Ephesians 5:14

Loving God is the mystical way to knowing God. And what is our reaction? – joy and gratitude. We sing God's praises joyfully, with loving devotion.

> Raise your voices in thanksgiving.
>
> Ephesians 5:5

> Sing the words and tunes of the psalms and hymns when
> you are together and go on singing and chanting to the
> Lord in your hearts...
>
> Ephesians 5:19-20

I like this St. Paul of the Ephesians. He is a very mystical fellow and surprisingly Eastern in his theology and his devotion to God.

The Mystical Body of Christ and Matthew 25

Matthew 25 is famous for multiple reasons, not the least of which it is the story of the Last Judgment. In the lengthy and somewhat repetitive story, Jesus divides us by the way we treat the least of our neighbors.

> For I was hungry, and you gave me food, I was thirst, and
> you gave me drink, I was naked, and you clothed me, sick
> and you visited me, and in prison, and you came to see me.
>
> Matthew 25:35-37

The other half did not. The surprise that come is when all those "I"s and "me"s are Jesus Christ:

> Whatever you do to the least of your brothers or sisters of
> mine, you do unto Me.
>
> Matthew 25

Then Jesus turns away from those who don't act compassionately toward the hungry, the thirsty, the naked, the sick, and those in prison, who may be the least of us, but still have Christ Consciousness residing in them. This is also a scary story as it implies a hellish outcome. *What if Jesus turns away from me at the Last Judgment?* This is, of course, "fear of the Lord," the beginning of Wisdom, the understanding that we will be held accountable for our actions.

This understanding of our relationship to God and our neighbor should be the moral basis not only of Christianity but all religions based in our true natures, the Dharma, the Truth. We are all members of Christ's (Buddha's, Shiva's, Sophia's) Mystical Body such that whatever we do to one another, we do to the Christ Consciousness, to God. In a sense, every action can be a prayer, or a curse, can it not?

God Is Heavily Invested in Each of Us

God gives us life and Consciousness, creates and sustains us, loves and cares for us. God wants us to have Communion with Him/Her. God wants us to know Him/Her intimately. God is very invested in people's lives and doesn't want people to be hurt or corrupted, certainly doesn't want people to be sacrificed in holocausts of war and suffering. One of the lessons of Jesus' crucifixion is God suffers for our sins.

The problem with the Self is Claiming You Are God

Because scripture refers to the Self as God inside everybody, we have people saying crazy things like, "I am God," or "We are God," or even "I am the universe." I look at these people from the perspective of Spock on *Star Trek* and reason, *The definition of God is that of a Person who is omniscient, omnipresent, and omnipotent, and you are none of these. Therefore, you are not God.* You need a spaceship. There are a few who don't need a spaceship, probably including Jesus and the Buddha, but most of the people you hear it from do. We think it is better to regard Enlightenment as a Baptism in Spirit in which we experience intimate knowledge of God. Because we recognize our consciousness intellectually overlaps God's Consciousness, it does not mean we are God from the human perspective but from God's perspective.

The witness to the human being not being God is the jerk: the wife beater, the drunk, the philanderer, the guy who cut me off in traffic, the guy arguing with me about religion saying he knows because he is God. You will note these examples always pick on the males, which gets to be a nuisance when you are Irish. The problem which St. Paul notes is the Self is "hidden" from both the observer and the person who is acting inappropriately. Thus, the Christ inside is hidden and we sure don't see Jesus in most, not even in ourselves. What we see are friends who can provide us with our wants and needs, or the jerks who can't

After reading over the Gospel, I think Jesus chose to die, breaking the law against blasphemy. We think Jesus is God but that is not the way the high priests and Roman governors saw Him. To them, Jesus was like everybody, zealot who made people mad by saying things He shouldn't. But that is not the way the high priests and Roman governors saw him. They saw Jesus as a regular human being and also a criminal. To them Jesus was just another oppositional religious zealot who made a lot of people mad by saying things he shouldn't.

Jesus Takes on the Role and Language of the Prophets

In the New Testament, Jesus identifies with the prophets and vehemently attacks the scribes and Pharisees, the Jewish scholars and social elite of that time. Like the prophets, Jesus was a harsh critic of the Jewish religious leadership of the time. In Jesus' parable about the cornerstone being rejected, we see Jesus criticize the high priests and scribes just like the prophets of old.

> "It was the stone rejected by the builders that became the keystone." He continued, "I tell you, then, that the kingdom of God will be taken from you and given to a people who will produce its fruit." When they heard his parables, the chief priests and the scribes realized he was speaking about them, but though they wanted to arrest Him, they were afraid of the crowds who looked on him as a prophet.
>
> Matthew 21: 42-43

We note the people regarded Jesus as a prophet and sided with Him against the religious elite. We note the prize that is taken away from the builders is the Kingdom of God, what we are to search for, the reason we seek Sophia.

Like the Prophets Jesus spoke religious truth to the religious authorities and insulted them directly. We remember how Isaiah harsh criticism of the temple priests from the chapter on the prophets' rebellion: "What are your endless sacrifices to me? I am sick of holocausts of rams and the fat of calves. The blood of bulls and goats revolts me." (Isaiah 1:11) Here is a sample of Jesus rebuke of the Scribes and Pharisees, the scholars and the elite of Jewish religious society of His time:

> Alas for you, Scribes and Pharisees, you hypocrites! You who shut up the Kingdom of God in men's faces, neither going in yourselves nor allowing others to go in who want to.
>
> Alas for you, Scribes and Pharisees, you hypocrites.

You who are like whitewashed tombs that look handsome on the outside, but inside are full of dead men's bones and every kind of corruption.

Serpents, brood of vipers, how can you escape being condemned to hell? This is why, in my turn, I am sending you prophets and wise men and scholars, some you will slaughter and crucify, some you will scourge in your synagogues, and hunt from town to town, and so you will draw down on yourselves the blood of every holy man that has been born down on earth. I tell you, all this will recoil on this generation.

Matthew, Chapter 9

"Whitewashed tombs ... Brood of vipers?" Jesus really knows how to hurl an insult. Here, Jesus attacks his opponents and invokes the dialectic of opposition. What is their sin? They "shut up the Kingdom of God in men's faces, neither going in yourselves nor allowing others to go in who want to." Clearly, Jesus is trying to open the gates of the Kingdom of God, while they try to shut it up in people's faces. If we translate finding the Kingdom of God as "Enlightenment," Jesus wants us to know God intimately, and the Scribes, Pharisees, and Temple priests don't. The Kingdom of God is where we recognize the presence of God in the world.

Jesus Uses the Wisdom Language and Parable Streams

Hopefully it is obvious to the reader that Jesus used the same language, metaphor, and parable streams developed in the Wisdom books of the Bible. What are we to do first? "Seek first the kingdom of God." We have shown how Jesus' parable stream was developed in the Wisdom books and from the Upanishads in previous chapters. In Wisdom we find we are to perceive God's presence in the world as Sophia, the Holy Spirit of Wisdom and Perception. She shows us the Kingdom of God. We remember Angela of Foligno crying out in chapter 13, "This whole world is full of God!"

St. John's Wisdom Gospels and Epistles

In discussing how Jesus and the Evangelists used the Wisdom language, we will be highlighting the works of St. John, which include his Gospel, his Epistles, and Revelations, and the mystical St. Paul of Ephesians and 1 Corinthians. Let us start with the prologue to St. John's Gospel, famous for its use of Wisdom words of deep meaning and spiritual metaphors.

> In the beginning was the Word;
> The Word was with God,
> And the Word was God.
> He was with God in the beginning.
> Through Him all things came to be,
> Not one thing came to be but through Him.
> All that came to be had Life in Him,
> And that Life was the Light of men,
> A Light that shines in the dark,
> A light that darkness cannot overpower.
> The word was the true Light
> Who Enlightens all humankind.
>
> John 1:1-5

This short passage is filled with the language of Wisdom with words of deep and mystical meaning written in poetic style and broken down by line and verse. In analyzing this passage, we remember that in Proverbs Sophia was "with God" at creation, and She "was (and still is) God." Sophia is the "giver of Life"; all "have Life" in the Word. Sophia is the Light that "shines in the darkness," the Light which "darkness cannot overcome," the Eternal Light. Sophia gives us "intimate knowledge of God"; here the True light "Enlightens all humankind."

However, the "He's" and "Him's" refer to Jesus Christ as the Word. What happened to Sophia? In the Wisdom books of the Bible written just before Jesus was born, it is fairly obvious that Sophia was the Word of God "who turns all things to good." In the prologue to St. John's Gospel in the Nicaea Creed, the Word became Jesus Christ. Constantine wanted Sophia to disappear, but can the reader see where She went, who She became?

If Sophia was the Word of God before Jesus was born, and the Word of God "took flesh and walked amongst us," it is logical Sophia the Holy Spirit of God took flesh and walked amongst us.

In the Creed it says that the Son, the second Person of the Trinity is "made of the same substance as the Father." Well, Jesus is made in part of flesh and bones. What of Jesus' essence might this divine substance be? The only thing I can think of is the Holy Spirit of God. If Jesus is divine, His essence, what we call His Soul, must be the Holy Spirit of God. And if you think about it, and the Holy Spirit of God must be the essential substance of God the Father, also. Thus, in whichever Person, the Father, the Son, or the Holy Spirit are all of one substance, the Holy Spirit of God. We have always known that were supposed to be of the same substance, but we never knew what they were talking about. Now we know. As St. John says, "God is Spirit."

Surprisingly, this interpretation has gained some approval amongst Christian scholars, who admit the idea Sophia "could be" or even "is" Jesus' soul. That is how She comes out of Him. They are actually One. I don't know how popular this interpretation is, but it is out there in even traditional Catholicism. The one caveat is, "Please don't make Sophia Pagan." But the best things in Christianity come from the Greeks and the East Indians, including Sophia.

The Word of God Enlightens

With Sophia, the Holy Spirit of Wisdom, comes Enlightenment, which is Her function, to Enlighten people. That is what Holy Wisdom is in the East. Enlightenment was recognized in Alexandria, Egypt, and confirmed by St. Augustine. Constantine wanted not only to get rid of Sophia but also Enlightenment – Communion with God, as an important goal for people to seek. Constantine needed mean soldiers to maintain his security, rich merchants to pay taxes to pay for the soldiers to protect him, and slaves to provide their labors for the greater glory of Rome. He certainly did not need the men of his realm to go off into the desert on this pie-in-the-sky search for Communion with God, or regard themselves to be loved by God, even be children of God. But just like Sophia, Enlightenment is right there in scripture, as big as day. We read quite clearly in St. John's Gospel, "The Word is the True Light who Enlightens all humankind." Enlightenment in the Wisdom Literature of the Bible, both Old Testament and New, is the same mystical experience of Enlightenment they have in the East. In scripture, both Jesus and Sophia Enlighten us. Most Christians do not recognize Enlightenment as a goal of Christianity, but that is Jesus' intention. If Jesus Enlightens us, has the reader asked Jesus to Enlighten them? When Sophia bids us to "Come drink the waters of Eternal Life for free," will you accept?

St. John Offers Us Eternal Life

In St. John, rather than seeking the "Kingdom of God," we are offered "Eternal Life." We remember "immortal bliss" in the Upanishad poem. I think we all fear death, having our bodies taken away, and long for immortality, for Eternal Life. Scripture answers this concern. Is Eternal Life available? Do we live on? How does one realize Eternal Life?

> Eternal life is this:
> To know you the One true God.
>
> John 17:3

The footnote to this passage in my Jerusalem Bible (48) states the form of "to know" used here is to know "in the Biblical sense," or "intimately." You gain Eternal Life through intimate Knowledge of the One God.

The Wisdom Story of the Woman at the Well

One of Jesus' teachings that best demonstrates the effectiveness of the language of Wisdom in engaging the reader is the story of the Woman at the well. The scene: While waiting at the community well, Jesus meets a Samaritan woman and asks her for a drink of water. She is surprised that He would ask her as she is a Samaritan and He is a Jew. But there is something quite attractive about her; she is inquisitive, open. As the conversation proceeds, Jesus offers her something much deeper than well water:

> Jesus:
> If you only knew what God is offering,

And who it is who is saying to you:

Give me a drink,

You would have been the one to ask,

And He would have given you living water.

Whoever drinks the water from this well

Will get thirst again;

But anyone who drinks the water that I shall give

Will never be thirsty again:

The water I shall give

Will turn into a spring inside you,

Welling up to eternal life.

"Sir," the woman responds, "Give me some water

So that I may never get thirsty."

John, Chapter 4

"Living Water..." What a wonderful metaphor for the life-giving Holy Spirit. "The water I shall give will turn into a spring inside you, welling up to eternal life."

If the well is inside us, where is it?

More than all else, keep watch over your heart,

Since here are the wellsprings of life.

Proverbs 4:23

It is the same in the East.

In the secret cave of the heart,

Two are seated by life's fountain.

Katha Upanishad (49)

The Samaritan woman is very lucky. Don't we all thirst for "Living Water?"

Jesus continues:

> You worship what you do not know;
> We worship what we do know;
> ... God is Spirit, and those who worship
> Must worship in Spirit and truth.
> John 4:21-24

It is interesting that Jesus says "we know" what we are talking about rather than "I know." It is also interesting that the St. John and the worshipers in his Epistles says the same thing: "We know what we are talking about" thus testifying to Jesus' and St. John's communities mystical knowledge. Perhaps the key word is worship as worship is done in a group. I would also note that this is also the way St. John words his statements in his Epistles – "We know what we are talking about." St. John also talks about being in "union" with God – what we might translate as "Union-Communion":

The "fountain of Living Water" is not only important because it is such a good metaphor for living Spirit but also because after being introduced in Songs, the theme follows through Jesus' ministry all the way to the last chapter of Revelations, where the Bride offers us the waters of Eternal Life famously for free.

> The Spirit and the Bride say, "Come."
> Let everyone who listens, answer, "Come."
> Then let all who are thirsty come:

All who want it may have the Water of Life, and have it free."

Revelations 22:17

I keep on coming back to this passage for a reason. Over and over we come back to this identity of the Spirit and the Bride and Her offer of the waters of Eternal Life.

St. John's Description of God

It seems like if you know God, you could describe God, and in order to demonstrate his knowledge of God, St. John states directly what God is:

God is Light.
1 John 1:5

They are of "the same substance" again, divine Light, divine Energy. This is how God is experienced, as the Eternal Light, as pure Life Energy, and this is why the experience of God is called Enlightenment.

Let us love one another, since love comes from God.

And everyone who loves is begotten by God and knows God.
Anyone who fails to love can never have known God,
Because God is Love.
1 John 4:7-8

God is Love. This is the overwhelming witness the mystics used to describe who God is in Enlightenment. God is Light; God is Love. This is universal around the world in those religions, allowing God to be active with us in the world.

It is also St. John who defines God as Spirit. This seems to be the substance that God is made of and how we experience Him/Her.

> God is Spirit, so those who worship Him must worship in Spirit and in truth.
>
> John 4:23-24

The Mystical St. Paul

The mystical St. Paul asks the Holy Spirit of Wisdom, Sophia, to bless us with full knowledge of God:

> May the God of our Lord Jesus Christ, the Father of Glory, give you the Holy Spirit of Wisdom and Perception of what is revealed, to bring you to full knowledge of God. May He Enlighten the eyes of your mind so that you can see what hope His call holds for you...
>
> Ephesians 1:17-19

St. Paul's "full knowledge of God" is Solomon's "Intimate Knowledge of God," which is St. John's Eternal Life, which is Communion with God or Enlightenment. From our reading, we know the "Holy Spirit of Wisdom and Perception" is Sophia. So right here in St. Paul's Epistle it says that Sophia, the Holy Spirit of Wisdom and Perception, gives us Enlightenment.

Jesus' Yoga is Easy

Perhaps we never thought of singing or loving God as religious practice. Singing is how we express our love for God and because it is joyful, it is easy. This is one way that Jesus is right when He says, "My yoke is easy." In the East, "yoga" is also derived from the verb "to yoke." In yoga we yoke our emotions and passions so that we can focus on God, live a happy life, and have intimate Knowledge of God. Jesus could be saying, "My yoga is easy." In the East, a yogi might meditate, fast, and pray for long periods of time. Jesus prayed in the desert for forty days and nights. But that does not seem "easy." It doesn't sound fun at all.

Meditation and Prayer

Did Jesus meditate? We know He prayed, and frankly, I see no difference between praying and saying a devotional mantra to God. If Jesus is out there in the desert for forty days and nights, just based on logic, I expect he used repetitive prayer. We note Syrian monks in the infancy of the Church used rosaries made of knotted rope, the same as the rosaries used in prior times by Indian yogis to count their mantra. We expect Jesus also used a rosary of knotted rope. Rosaries were invented in India and are still used by Hindus today to count mantras. Some Muslims also use rosaries to count their prayers because of prior contacts with the Indian meditation tradition.

Loving God is the Way

So although some of the disciplines Jesus undertook seem "hard," the most important aspect of Jesus' yoke or yoga, His spiritual practice is easy because it is based on loving God. And loving God "with all our hearts, minds, souls, and with all our strength" is Jesus' Greatest Commandment. Loving God is also the mystical method by which we know God and find we are all members of Christ's Mystical Body. Loving God as Sophia is the best way to seek and find Her.

Jesus Empowers Sophia's Sacraments

I was surprised when I read Sophia introduced the Eucharistic meal in Proverbs. "Come eat my bread and drink the wine I have prepared." This may puzzle some people who thought Jesus instituted the sacramental meal. But even early theologians knew that philosophical mystery cults also served Eucharistic Meals. We also know there were mystery sects in Alexandria, Egypt, during the Late Greek period, and there were mystery sects active during Jesus' lifetime. In the Gospel of St. Thomas, there are indications that Jesus was a participant, perhaps a master, of these rituals. We can't say that the words Sophia said at Her Eucharistic meal were the same as Jesus,' but I expect they were close.

But Sophia is not limited to the Eucharist in Her connection to sacramental rites. As the Holy Spirit of Wisdom, She is directly involved in all the sacraments, but especially in the sacraments of initiation. In Baptism we are "reborn in the Holy Spirit" of Wisdom and Perception. In Confirmation we are to receive the Holy Spirit through a laying on of hands of an Enlightened Bishop. In the Holy Eucharist, we are introduced to the mystery of the Mystical Body of Christ and discover we are part of Christ's body.

Sophia's parables and sacraments are designed to change our perception of the universe, of the world we live in, and to include God's presence. We must make a jump in our understanding that changes the way we see things. "This is my Body." Then you eat Christ's body and what do you become? The hard part is figuring out how the bread can possibly be part of God's body.

The Marriage of the Christ and Sophia

But in my mind, the way to document Jesus' affirmation of Sophia is His marriage to Sophia. In the Gospel of St. John, John the Baptist explains using the well-developed Wisdom metaphor of marriage of Lover and Beloved:

> The Bride is only for the Bridegroom;
> And yet the Bridegroom's friend,
> Who stands there and listens,
> Is glad when he hears the Bridegroom's voice,
> The same joy I feel, and now it is complete.
>
> John 3:29

Jesus is the Groom, but to whom? Based on some romantic book accounts, the bride was Mary Magdalene. But that doesn't fit the scene, and they weren't married anyway, were they? Yet, marriage is a well-developed metaphor for Communion with God in the Wisdom tradition of the Old Testament. In Wisdom, Solomon falls in love with Sophia and vows to marry Her. Then there is the marriage of Lover and Beloved in the Song of Songs. Especially given it is John's Wisdom Gospel, I think John was talking metaphorically. Jesus is married to Sophia. The metaphorical meaning of their marriage is they are in intimate Communion, They are One. They are married, just like Shiva and Shakti at the Hindu cave temples at Elphanta and Ellora that Pythagoras visited. The marriage of the Christ and the Holy Spirit of Wisdom is an obvious metaphor in the Wisdom tradition. This marriage, or Communion, symbolizes Christ Consciousness merged with the energy and power of God – the macro Holy Spirit – as the universe.

When we realize that Jesus and Sophia come as a happily married couple and of the same divine substance, Holy Spirit, we begin to understand Jesus' real message, what He wanted for us, what He showed us, and what we can accomplish. Christianity is steeped in the mystical experience of God, and always has been. Christianity is not all rules. Jesus wanted to bring the joy of Communion with God to humankind.

The Schism Between Eastern and Western Religion is Healed in Sophia

As Christ's Mystical Body unites Pagan, Greek, and Jew in One Body, Sophia the Holy Spirit unites East and West. Hinduism, Yoga, and philosophy have long been the source of inspiration in the West. We need no longer consider philosophy bad, or Hinduism Pagan. It is from them we learned about the Holy Spirit of Wisdom, Hagia Sophia.

> Thousands of years ago, before Moses or Buddha or Christ, sages stood on India's river banks and sang songs inspired, the Hindus say, "by the Breath of God." Out of these chants and out of the wisdom and spirituality of the sages in the centuries since has grown the religions known today as Hinduism …. The followers believe that Hinduism, the origins of which go back 4,000 years, is not only the oldest of all religions but the fountainhead of all; without question it has influenced Western thought indirectly for centuries. Pythagoras and Neo-Platonists studied it;

Schopenhauer and Emerson were certainly stimulated by it; the Mahatma Gandhi won worldwide reverence for his practice of Hindu nonviolence.

The World's Great Religions (50)

"The Breath of God..." Where have we heard that? We hope you recognize the Breath of God to be Sophia. In Wisdom Christianity we come into a new theological paradigm where Western Christians can now share in the mystical adventure of knowing God intimately through the teachings of Jesus Christ and Sophia. Kipling was wrong in his judgment that "East is East and West is West and never the twain shall meet." Now the East and West have met, and through knowledge of Sophia, we are healed in one Body, the Body of Christ, which is known by different names, the Body of Buddha, the Body of Shiva, but are just different names for God.

Chapter Sixteen: *St. Basil the Great*

St. Basil the Great Saves and Defines the Holy Spirit, Like Sophia, but Male

St. Basil The Great and the Cappadocia Fathers

The values of the Early Christian Church were compromised by imperial Rome, and Sophia, the Holy Spirit of Wisdom, was assigned to the dust bin of history. Well, the Sophia part went away but there was still a Holy Spirit that was initially left undefined. The original draft copy of the Nicene Creed merely states Her existence: "We believe in… the Holy Spirit." Basil contributed to early Christian liturgy and prayer, established the Christian monastic system, established hospitals to care for the sick, and shelters to feed the poor, but his greatest contribution was his definition of the Holy Spirit as equal to and of the same substance as the Father and the Son.

The initial Nicene Creed focused on God the Father and the divinity of Jesus Christ. The Holy Spirit was mentioned as a matter of faith but was not described. In the final Nicene Creed, the Holy Spirit is much better defined as a divine person who is active in the world. If you ignore the Holy Spirit's gender and non-descript personality, you can recognize the qualities of Sophia shining through.

Basil was a very gifted leader amongst an extraordinary community of Christians who effectively saved mystical Christianity in the West. The Cappadocia Fathers consisted of Basil, his brother Gregory Nyssa, bishop of Nyssa, and Gregory of Naziazus, a close friend of Basil's, who later became Patriarch of Constantinople. They are grouped among the early "Fathers of the Church."

Not exactly a "Father" of the Church, but someone else who had an enormous impact on Christianity was Macrina, Basil's sister. She seems to have kept the group centered and focused on a firm commitment to Christ's message. Macrina later established the first woman's monastery. In fact, over time the family estate became a monastery, with an attached hospital and homeless shelter to serve the poor, as Jesus advocated in the gospels. It seems while the men were promoted to leadership positions in the Church and kept quite busy, Macrina kept the home, the hospital, and monasteries running.

Basil Developed the Theology of the Holy Spirit

In his youth, Basil was well educated and well traveled. Historians have Basil meeting Gregory in Caesaria in what is now Turkey, and while Gregory later went to Alexandria, Basil went to Constantinople, the capital of the Eastern Roman Empire. Then Basil traveled to Athens and met Gregory where they become fast friends. We note the continuing importance of Alexandria, Athens, and now Constantinople, in higher education circles. Basil later traveled to Egypt and Syria to study with the ascetic hermits at the early monasteries there.

Based on Basil's and the Cappadocia Fathers' work, the Holy Spirit was portrayed and defined as follows at the Council of Constantinople:

- Jesus was "conceived" by the Holy Ghost.
- The Holy Spirit is the "Lord and Giver of Life."

- The Holy Spirit is to be "adored and glorified as the Father and the Son."
- The Holy Spirit "spoke through the prophets."
- The Holy Spirit "proceeds from the Father and the Son." I would note here that the interpretation of this line proved controversial and in part caused the schism between the Eastern and Western Christianities

Like Sophia in the Wisdom books of the Bible, the Holy Spirit of the final Nicene Creed is "the Giver of Life." Like Sophia, the Holy Spirit spoke through the prophets, emanated from the transcendent God as the Power and Energy of God, but most importantly perhaps, the Holy Spirit is to be "adored and glorified as the Father and the Son." Is not love and devotion to the Holy Spirit the best way to knowing Sophia intimately?

Should we care if the Holy Spirit is male rather than female? As indicated earlier, when we think of God as "Lord" and "Law Giver," as the final authority, we think of a male image. If we define God as Love, as it does in scripture, then we tend to think of God as Mother for the simple reason that when asked who loves us most, we typically say our mothers. I prefer a woman Holy Spirit if for no other reason that it brings some balance in our image of God and permits the marriage of Christ and Sophia. But you could also say a male Holy Spirit can love you as much as a female Holy Spirit, and is the Holy Spirit being male all that big a deal? It is Sophia's allure, Her personality, Her attractiveness I miss, and Her invitation. Women in monasteries have regarded Jesus Christ as their Beloved since the beginning of the women's monastic movement. For Solomon and Jesus, both males, Sophia was their marriage partner. Through Sophia, men have a Lover in God that woman have enjoyed in

Jesus for centuries. In India, they tell you to love the form of God you love the most. I love Sophia and miss Her in our theology and worship. Returning Sophia to Her rightful place as the Holy Spirit of Wisdom can usher in a Renaissance of Spirit in both Judaism and Christianity.

Basil Faced Deadly Opposition

We all take the Holy Spirit and Nicene Creed as fairly standard Christian theology. What we find surprising is the opposition that Basil incurred even with this Biblically supported description of the Holy Spirit. Basil was opposed and his life threatened by the authoritarian imperialist prelates and governors, who wanted to impose their culture and laws on the church. St. Basil regarded this argument a life-threatening war.

> But preparations for war against us has been made, every thought is aimed at us, and the tongues of the blasphemers shoot arrows at us and hit us more vehemently than the Christ-slayers hit Stephen with stones.
>
> On the Holy Spirit (51)

Please note that Basil's enemies were not opposed to the Holy Spirit just because of gender. The Holy Spirit Basil was proposing was the traditional male version. Basil's opponents resented the idea that sinful human beings could have union Communion with God.

> Why must we shamefully gain a victory in argument by fighting for such trifles, when it is possible to prove in a more dignified way that the exceeding glory cannot be

> denied. Now if we should say that we have been taught
> by scriptures, they will cry out swiftly, exceedingly, and
> excessively; they will shut their ears and hurl stones at us
> – or whatever each of the Spirit-fighters can make into a
> weapon. In truth, we must not honor our personal safety
> over the truth.
>
> On the Holy Spirit (52)

"...the exceeding glory cannot be denied." We remember Sophia is the image of God's glory? In his letters, St. Basil explains the source of his conviction for his definition of the Holy Spirit. Basil, like Solomon, like St. Paul, was graced with full knowledge of God:

> Am I to be turned aside by their arguments of plausibility
> and to surrender the tradition that leads me to the Light and
> that has graced me with the Knowledge of God, through
> which I have been received as a child of God?
>
> On the Holy Spirit (53)

Basil describes his experience.

> Just like the sun, [the Holy Spirit] will use the eye that
> has been cleansed to show you in Himself the image of
> the invisible, and in the blessed vision of the image you
> will see the unspeakable beauty of the archetype. Through
> this comes the ascent of hearts, the guidance of the weak,
> and the perfection of those making progress. The Spirit
> illuminates [Enlightens] those who have been cleansed

from every stain and makes them spiritual by means of Communion with Himself.

On the Holy Spirit (54)

Although there are a lot of Greek words that clouds what Basil is saying, Basil knows the qualities of the Holy Spirit because Basil experienced "Him." The Holy Spirit Enlightened Basil. Basil had intimate Knowledge of God, and Basil does a good job describing the experience. According to Basil's witness then, the traditional Christian Church should acknowledge the Holy Spirit Enlightens us, gives us intimate knowledge of and Communion with God. St. Basil the Great is a fantastic example of Christianity's potential, what Christianity could be.

Chapter Seventeen: Mary as Divine Mother

Jesus' Mother Mary Becomes Our Spiritual Mother

During its early years, the Christian Church absorbed the holidays, sacramental rites, liturgy, and "saints" of the pre-existing Pagan religion. Christmas is a good example. We don't know the exact date of Jesus' birth. It was set at 25 December as that was when many celebrated the winter solstice and the re-birth of the sun. God as Mother was celebrated in Pagan Rome and throughout the empire before Christianity was institutionalized as the Roman Catholic Church. When God became all male and Christianity was the approved church of the Roman Empire, many missed the divine feminine, as we do today. Due to popular demand, the Roman Catholic Church held the Council of Ephesus in 431 AD and elevated the ever Virgin Mary to the vaunted position of "the Mother of God." That was pretty much the sole purpose of the Ecumenical Council, to establish a Mother to pray to. Ever since, the church has promoted Mother Mary as the "Queen of Heaven," "Ever Virgin" (meaning pure and holy like Sophia), "Immaculately Conceived," and "Assumed into Heaven" like Jesus. She became the universal Mother of us all because we are all members of Christ's Mystical Body, and since Mary gave birth to Jesus, Mary is our mystical mother.

During my childhood, the Virgin Mary was the go-to person if you wanted or needed something from God. A grade-school nun explained:

"Jesus and God the Father might be busy managing the universe, so you want to pray to an insider like Jesus' Mother, and she will put in a good word for you." This also gives an interesting perspective on family life during that time.

Earlier, I remarked that I could not remember learning any prayers to say to the Holy Spirit. But, in retrospect, I said more prayers to Mother Mary than any other prayer, including the Our Father, so I was praying to the (almost) divine Mother all the time. The Hail Mary prayer goes like this:

> Hail Mary, full of Grace,
> The Lord is with thee.
> Blessed art thou amongst women,
> And blessed is the fruit of thy womb, Jesus.
> Holy Mary, Mother of God,
> Pray for us sinners now
> And at the hour of our death.
>
> Amen

Directly addressing the Mother of God, with "Hail Mary" is the style of the Stoic philosophers that I borrowed for the Hail Sophia. I think it's important that we address our Mother directly, hail her, and regard Her as present.

The Hail Mary prayer is short and catchy, and I still say it to myself from time to time, especially when thinking about the last line ... "at the hour of our death." It would be nice to have Mother Mary or Sophia, or someone loving that we know, to help us through the transformation of death, to take us to the other side.

It is perhaps important to note that this portrayal of Mary as Mother of God is an idealized version of Mary. The Mary of the Gospel was quite human, and there was conflict even within the holy family. We remember in the Bible when Mary is standing outside the public house calling for Jesus, and He refuses her saying that He was with His "real family now." Although we pay little attention to this side of Jesus and His relationship with His family, knowing of the tension dividing Jesus and Mary adds emotional drama to the scene at the base of the cross where Jesus and His mother are reunited.

But was Mary, the Mother of Jesus, ever virgin? I expect being ever virgin was primarily a metaphor for being pure of heart. Purity is an important quality of God's love. For humans, blessed are the pure of heart, for they will see God. (Beatitudes) Was the human Mary ever virgin? I think it more possible than most would think, but there are credible claims out of India that such does on occasion occur, but it is difficult to prove, and I really don't care. This is not amongst the things I worry about.

Rosaries Are Linked to the Worship of Mother Mary

Rosaries are closely associated with the worship of Mother Mary. When Catholics say the rosary, they repeat ten Hail Marys to each Our Father. While praying "Hail Marys," we are actually thinking or meditating on the Mysteries of the Rosary, which are different scenes in Jesus' life. I prefer the Glorious Mysteries of the rosary. I regard the sorrowful mysteries to be a bit morbid and designed to illicit guilt rather than love. The root word of these "mysteries" we meditate on is "mystos," which relates this style of meditation to "mysticism." The repetition of the "Hail Marys" is counted on a rosary just like yogis count their prayers on their rosaries.

After Rome fell, the Roman Catholic Church was centered in the eastern half of the Empire. We remember this as the same region from which the Cappadocia fathers, including Basil, originated. Basil's sister, Macrina, established the monastic tradition for women at the same time Basil established the male tradition. We expect Macrina and her monastic followers had an important role in the elevation of Mother Mary as our almost divine Mother and in Her worship on rosaries, meditating on mysteries that demonstrate the actions of the Word of God in the world.

Litanies to the Mother

Litanies are another means of devotion common to Mother Mary, Sophia, and the Wisdom Mother of India. Here is a portion of the litany to the Catholic Mother Mary, describing her glory and purity, and asking Her to pray for us:

Leader: Holy Virgin of virgins,
Response: "Pray for us."

Mother most pure,	Mother of good council,
Mother of our Creator,	Mother of our Savior,
Virgin most powerful,	Mirror of justice,
Seat of Wisdom,	Cause of our joy,
Mystical rose,	Tower of ivory,
Ark of the Covenant,	Gate of heaven,
Morning star,	Queen of prophets,
Queen of the holy rosary,	Queen of peace,

Litany of the Blessed Virgin Mary (55)

This is but a sample of Mary's titles. The list goes on, and one can look up the rest of the litany on the internet. These are similar to descriptive litanies of the East and highlight similarities to Sophia. For example, did you know that the Virgin Mary was "most powerful?" We remember Sophia as "the power of God." Mary is the "Seat of Wisdom," as is Sophia. Both are "ever pure," Mary by being ever virgin.

Litanies to the Wisdom Mother are Popular in India

Litanies were used in India in ancient times and are still used today to describe the Wisdom Mother's purity and attractiveness. Hindu litanies to the Wisdom Mother vary in length from one short litany of four lines to a thousand and one names of the Holy Mother. Although these attributes can change depending on the litany, there is a great deal of overlap between the description of Sophia, Mother Mary, and the Wisdom Mother of India. Throughout this discourse we have heard all of the metaphors and concepts used to describe Sophia, Jesus, or Mother Mary in this Hindu litany to the Wisdom Mother.

The Wisdom Mother is ...

Consciousness itself,	Supreme bliss,
She who abides in the heart,	She who grants Enlightenment,
Full of motherly love,	Holy Wisdom,
Attained by meditation,	Eternal joy and happiness,
Ever pure, the Truth, Eternal,	God (divine),
Mother of the universe,	She who gives salvation,
Knower of all thoughts,	She who is attained through devotion

The Thousand Names of the Divine Mother (56)

I won't go over these titles individually, but they are worthy of individual consideration and contemplation. It is notable that the Wisdom Mother, Sophia, and Mother Mary are "ever pure." That is what Mary's virginity signifies metaphorically.

Marian Apparitions

Isn't it interesting that Mother Mary still makes appearances to her devotees on earth? As a kid, I was into visitations of the Virgin Mary and read about her at Fatima and Mother Mary's mysterious message to the Pope. But then for a long time I didn't believe in miracles and forgot about these mysterious appearances. But now that I have friends who are visited by Jesus in their dreams, while gurus and saints are making "appearances" to modern American Hindus, apparitions of Mother Mary seem fun again. I have a picture or our Lady of Guadeloupe on the wall of the study next to pictures of the Wisdom Mother of India and Sophia.

Chapter Eighteen: *Spiritual Practice*

Meditating on Sophia

The next step is practice. Jesus said seek the Kingdom of God first, before we do anything else. Practice is a verb, something we do. We started out on the cover saying "Happy are they who meditate on Sophia." So after prayer, the next steps in seeking Sophia meditating on Sophia.

Here at the Jim McG Forest School of Philosophy we are not trying to establish a new religion but to re-open the latent channels of spiritual Wisdom and our connection with Hagia Sophia, Holy Spirit of Wisdom in the Judeo-Christian tradition. Christianity is a very diverse religious tradition, containing all sorts of sects differentiating themselves by dogma, cultural roots, and attitude towards God and humankind. Christianity contains both Baptists and anabaptists. The Baptists believe you must be baptized in the Holy Spirit to enjoy Eternal Life. The Anabaptists include meditative Quakers, who think baptismal rites are just a Christening ceremony, just pomp and circumstance, and that we should seek God's Word in silence. And generally, most Christians get along now without saying the other side will go to hell because they don't believe in such and such. But then it is also wise to choose who you discuss some topics with.

From the Wisdom perspective, true (Dharmic) Christianity is quite simple. You do what Jesus tells you to do first: Seek first the Kingdom of God. That takes you on the whole seeking and finding metaphor stream till you find Sophia, the Holy Spirit of Wisdom and Perception, who gives us perception of the Kingdom of God. And then we follow the Greatest Commandment: Love God with all your heart, mind and soul, and your neighbor as your Self. Although this takes much skill in dealing with the "naked ape" neighbor who doesn't know he is God and judges based on his instincts, God wants us to get along. The basis of Christian morality is we are all member of Christ's Mystical Body, such that whatever we do to the least of our neighbors, (even the jerk) we do to Christ Consciousness, who knows all.

In this diverse Judeo-Christian tradition there, is certainly for the star of the Wisdom books of the Bible, Hagia Sophia, to shine brighter. Let us allow the worship and adoration of a female Holy Spirit as it is clearly stated in scripture and built into our language. Spirit is feminine in Aramaic and Hebrew, neuter in Greek, but Hagia Sophia, the Holy Spirit of Wisdom, is certainly feminine per our Bibles. There is Enlightenment; it is also in the Bible: "The Word is the True Light who Enlightens all humankind." Enlightenment is to be sought after, pursued. As we have been arguing that Jesus and the Holy Spirit are of one substance, they are both the Word, but in Enlightenment we have Communion in Spirit.

Meditation and prayer are individual practices. You can do them at home, you can do them in church, you can do them in the forest, you can remember God on your way to work in traffic, but it is hard to do while watching the TV. Although the encouragement of an authoritative bishop or priest helps, it is not necessary. Just as we form book clubs and prayer groups at church, we can start meditation groups and read about Sophia in our book clubs. Given the choices of what Person of God to worship,

Sophia is certainly to be adored and glorified as the Father and the Son. Maybe She likes to be adored and glorified even more than the Father and the Son because She is a She. Anyway, once you get to know Her, it comes naturally. She just deserves it, She is so beautiful.

I think once people find out about Sophia, She will enter into Christianity by osmosis. Just as many Christians believe in karma and reincarnation, we can believe in Sophia as Mother or Bride. Christianity is now a world phenomenon, and now that we know it is possible, we want a divine Mother, and we want intimate knowledge of Sophia, the Holy Spirit of Wisdom. Who is to stop us if that is what God wants too.

In order to meditate on Sophia we need to have some idea of what Sophia is like, who She is. She is described fairly well as a very attractive Person in the Wisdom books of the Bible as you know after reading the book. To focus the mind on who you are meditating on, we recommend you begin your meditation after reading the "Hail Sophia" prayer at the beginning of the book, or another devotional prayer to the image of God you love the most.

Sophia is the Biblical image of God as the divine feminine. She is the love and giver of Life we long for in God. She is a fountain of the waters of Eternal Life. She is the Breath and Glory of God. Yah, I think over time Sophia will catch on because She is such a great Person to know and love.

Prayer as a Founding Act of Faith

When my dad told me that God loved me and could hear my prayers, I believed Him. He also said that God might intercede on my behalf in troubled times, and I'm sure He did in a couple instances, but not at others. That's karma. We are supposed to learn from experience, even from previous lifetimes, but we are slow learners.

A Meditation on Sophia

Since the Forest School is promoting meditation on Sophia, we better offer a meditation on Sophia because we don't see many around currently.

This is an Eastern style meditation, a visualization associated with a short mantra, a line of a prayer. The meditator is asked to respond to the image of God emotionally, with love and devotion. In meditation you focus on the subject repeatedly, each time deepening focus on meaning and understanding, deepening reality of the Light and Love that She is. I know of many people, many friends who tried meditation and quit because it was boring. This is not an uncommon complaint among meditators of all religious persuasions. The story goes like this: A Buddhist monk complains to his master that just thinking of breathing is boring. So the master grabs him and dunks his head under water until he almost drowned. "Now is just breathing boring?" the master demands. Most would prefer not to be dunked under water but be given a more positive, maybe even glorious object to meditate upon. After years of meditating in different styles, we find devotional meditation is the easiest form to use because Sophia is so attractive, so devotion to Her comes naturally. She is gloriously beautiful by Her very nature, and given She loves us, She is very easy to love back. Note, the object of this meditation is to love Sophia with all your heart, mind, and soul. What can be better, more romantic, more fulfilling than falling in love with the beautiful Being who is the glory of God?

The following beginning meditation is based on a famous Eastern mantra or short prayer, the Gayatri Mantra. It is a devotional mantra devoted to Devi, the Wisdom Mother of the East. As Sophia represents the Wisdom Mother in the West, She is also "Devi." The Gaytri Mantra is short, consisting of four lines, of which we will be using only one. Like the Wisdom books of the Bible, the Gaytri Mantra is filled with imagery and metaphor and words of deep meaning. You can read all the different ways it has been translated on the internet. I will provide a translation suitable for meditation on Sophia/Devi.

The Gaytri Mantra consists of four lines:

> Ohm Bhur bhuvah svah
> Tat Savitur verenyam
> Bhargo Devasya dhimahi
> Dhiyo yo nah prachodayat
>
> Rig Veda (57)

Sanskrit is one of the Indo-European languages, so the pronunciation is phonetic, but not always. I find it interesting that both the Latin Catholics and the Hindus of India claim the sounds of their language are tuned to the spiritual nervous system. This verse can be sung, and there are great recordings on the Internet. The version by Deva Premal is well performed and famous. The problem is that most Judeo-Christians do not know Sanskrit; most of us think in English. On the other hand, the words are not all that different "Tat," meaning "That" is an example, but Tat has the additional meaning of "That which is divine."

The Gayatri Mantra starts with *Ohm,* the primal sound vibrating through creation, introducing the prayer. The first line names the different realms – the physical, the mental, and the spiritual realms of creation, and acknowledges the beings that inhabit these realms. The next line is key and our focus:

Tat Savitur Varenyam

"Tat" is "That," but capitalized so that it can be translated mentally as, "That which is divine." With "Savitur" we think of the image of the "Sun rise of Sophia," the giver of Life and Light. Verenyam is a long word in Sanskrit so I just say "Perfect" here and admire Sophia, the sunrise, and the sparkling glory of the sun dancing of the water as a Being, as Sophia.

After we complete our visualization, we then express our love of Sophia, adore Her, and entreat Sophia to Enlighten our minds. As a whole, the Gayatri Mantra is a very good prayer to Devi so the devotee may want to add the entire poem to their prayer repertoire.

Steps in the Meditation

So the steps of our Meditation on Hagia Sophia are as follows.

1. Take three deep breaths, chant three deep "Ohm" silently in the mind. Feel the energy of the vibration filling both your body and the space around you.
2. Breath in and out, "That divine Sunrise of Sophia" while visualizing a beautiful sunrise with the sunlight dancing off the water in radiant glory. Recognize that energy of God to be the Glory of God, the Goodness of God, Sophia, a Person, a Being. Breath in and out, recognizing Her as the source, the metaphorical sun radiating Love.
3. Reflect on Sophia's glory: "Perfect." Give yourself time, a breath or two, to feel and admire the light and grace that radiates out of

Sophia, the source of spiritual Light, Life, and Grace.

4. Respond to Sophia's grace and love by returning Her love. Tell Her you Love Her, cherish Her presence, and adore Her Being for three breaths. As your love for Sophia can become quite intimate, tell Her in your own way, simply, for three breaths. "I love you Sophia."

Those who haven't watched a sunrise or sunset recently, may want to take some time off and sit on the banks of a river, stream, lake, or ocean and watch the sun rise slowly over the water, casting jewels of light dancing on the waters. Taking time for sunrises might be your first step in appreciating what just a drop of God's glory is worth.

Joyful Devotion to God Supercharges Our Love for God

It is important in the meditation and prayer to invoke the emotions of love and devotion for Sophia. The fountain of spirit resides in the heart, and love pours out. Adore Her in meditation and when you remember Her. Remember She is always there with you; She is omniscient and knows everything.

In India they include devotional singing of mantras and names of God as a means to express their love for God. Chanting God's names in the East to singing Psalms in early Christianity, lets God hear of our love for God. If it is by love of Sophia that we find Her, what better way to adore Her than singing to Her. "God's Love is all there is."

By singing, we open up our hearts and express your love for God with all our hearts, minds, souls, and with all of our strength, just like it says in the Greatest Commandment. In India, when you have "Kevala Bhakti" or total love for God, you are in Communion with God as Love.

Epilogue: A Beginning

Sophia Makes Us an Offer We Can't Refuse

After reading this book, hopefully you know something that you did not know before. Now what do you do with the information? There is an opportunity here that perhaps you did not know was there before. Maybe Her story makes sense, and you find Sophia attractive, like someone you want to get to know.

Now that you know Sophia as the Holy Spirit of Wisdom, think of how close Christianity becomes to being a truly remarkable vehicle for forming a real and permanent relationship with God. With Sophia, the Judeo-Christian tradition is born again without imperial dressings and instead, emphasizing our mystical opportunity to have real Union-Communion with God. I hold up Basil not only as a remarkable intellect but as an even more remarkable Christian and practitioner of his faith with the wisdom to know what God wants, including caring for the sick, and feeding the poor, devoting one's life to prayer in his monastery glorifying and adoring Sophia. With Sophia as the Holy Spirit of Wisdom and Perception, Judaism and Christianity once again works. The channels of Spirit and the intimate experience of God in Enlightenment open.

To conclude our lessons, let us end as we began this book with the final invitation of Sophia at the end of the Bible, the epilogue of Revelations. Here Sophia appears in Her Biblical roles as the Bride and Spirit, and offers us the waters of Eternal Life, for free:

> The Spirit and the Bride say, "Come."
> Let everyone who listens answer, "Come."
> Then let all who are thirsty come:
> All who want it may have the Water of Life,
>> And have it free.
>
> Revelations 22:17

Who can turn down such a wonderful invitation from the gloriously attractive Sophia, the image of God's Goodness, the Eternal Light that outshines the sun? And besides, intimate Communion with God is what Sophia wants too. Doesn't everyone want the Water of Eternal Life? And it's free!

Endnotes:

1. Dr. Karen Armstrong, *A History of God* (New York: Glamercy Books, 1993), p. 47.

2. Bishop John Shelby Spong, *Why Christianity Must Change or Die: A Bishop Speaks to Believers in Exile* (San Francisco: HarperOne, 1998), Reference to title.

3. Stacy Schiff, *Cleopatra, a Life* (New York: Little Brown and Company, 2010), p. 34.

4. Ed. Times Books Ltd, *The Times Atlas of World History* (London: Times Books Limited, 1984) p. 70.

5. Alexander Jones General Editor, *Jerusalem Bible* (New York: Doubleday & Company 1966) Introduction to the book of Holy Wisdom.

6. Armstrong, *A History of God*, p. 69.

7. Armstrong, *A History of God*, p. 47.

8. Eknath Easwaran, *The Upanishads* (Lilgiri Press 1987, Blue Mountain Center of Meditation 2007, Tomales, CA) p. 57, Isha Upanishad.

9. Editors, *Jerusalem Bible*, Introduction to the Song of Songs.

10. Easwaran, *The Upanishads,* p. 112, Forest Upanishad.

11. Daniel Ladinsky, *Love Poems from God* (London, Penguin Books, 2002) p. 187.

12. Editors, *Jerusalem Bible*, footnote to Songs 5:6.

13. Thomas Stanley, *Pythagoras: His Life and Teachings; A Compendium of Classical Sources* (Lake Worth, Fl, Ibis Press, 2010) p. 24.

14. "Wikipedia," Article "Elephanta Caves," (10/2021).

15. L. Hixon, *Great Swan; Meetings with Ramakrishna* (Larson Publications for the Paul Brunton Philosophic Foundation 1992, 1996) p. 73.

16. C. M. Bowra and Editors of Time Life, *Classical Greece, Great Ages of Man Series*, (New York, Time Life, 1965) p 159.

17. Livius.Org, "Articles on Ancient History," (Internet 10/2022).

18. John Keay, *India, A History*, (New York, Grove Press 2000, 2010) pgs. 70-71.

19. "Wikipedia," "Alexander the Great/ Indian Campaign of Alexander the Great," (October 2021).

20. Wikipedia, "Alexander the Great," (Oct. 2021).

21. Paramahansa Yogananda, *Autobiography of a Yogi* (Los Angeles, CA Self Realization Fellowship 13th Edition) pgs. 427-430 Comment: I first found this lengthy excerpt in Yogananda's Autobiography and will give him credit here so that people read him. However, Yogananda took this passage from an earlier work by McCrindle: *Ancient India as Described by Megasthenes and Arian* published in 1897. McCrindle's book was reissued 1927. It is available on Openware, (Archive.org) and in Google Books.

22. Yogananda, *Autobiography of a Yogi*, p. 430.

23. Wikipedia article, "Ashoka" (10/2021).

24. Yogananda, *Autobiography of Yogi* (New York, Philosophical Library Edition, 1946), p. 370.

25. Karen Armstrong, *The Great Transformation*; (Anchor Books 2007), p. xix.

26. Stacy Schiff, *Cleopatra*, p. 22.

27. Karen Armstrong, *A History of God*, p. 47.

28. Wikipedia, article "Ptolemy VIII," (August 2022).

29. Easwaran, *The Upanishads*, p. 13, Chandogya Upanishad.

30. Easwaran, *The Upanishads*, p. 77, Katha Upanishad.

31. Easwaran, *The Upanishads*, p. 114, Forest Upanishad.

32. Easwaran, *The Upanishads*, p. 115, Forest Upanishad.

33. Easwaran, *The Upanishads*, p. 126, Chandogyo Upanishad.

34. Easwaran, *The Upanishads*, p. 194, Mundaka Upanishad.

35. Robert W. Funk, Roy W. Hoover, and the Jesus Seminar, *The Five Gospels: The Search for the Authentic Words of Jesus* (Harper San-Fransisco,1993).

36. Marvin Meyer and Harold Bloom, *The Gospel of St. Thomas: The Hidden Sayings of Jesus* (New York, HarperCollins Publishers, 1992) p. 55.

37. Meyer and Bloom, *The Gospel of St. Thomas*, p. 113.

38. Editors Willis Barnstone and Marvin Meyer, *The Gnostic Bible*, includes the Gospel of Mary Magdalene, (Boston and London, Shambala Press, 2003, 2009).

39. Andrew Harvey, *Teachings of Christian Mystics* (Boston, Shambhala Pocket Library, 1997) p. 88.

40. Easwaran, *The Upanishads*, Pgs. 143-144, Chandogya Upanishad.

41. Easwaran, *The Upanishads*, p. 112, Forest Upanishad.

42. Easwaran, *The Upanishads*, p. 141-142, Chandogya Upanishad.

43. Harvard Classics, Volume: *Bacon, Milton, Brown*, (New York, P. F. Collier and Son 1909) The Essays of Francis Bacon. p. 11.

44. Israel Finkelstein and Neil Asher Silberman, *The Bible Unearthed* (New York and London, Touchstone/ Simon and Schuster, 2001), Chapters on "Did the Exodus Happen" and "Conquest of Canaan." From the back of the book: "(the authors) argue that crucial evidence (or telling lack of evidence) at digs in Israel, Egypt, Jordan, and Lebanon suggests that many of the most famous stories in the Bible – the wanderings of the patriarchs, the Exodus from Egypt, Joshua's conquest of Canaan, the David and Solomon's vast empire – reflect the world of the later authors rather than actual historical facts." Generally, this is admitted amongst scholars but rarely stated from the pulpit.

45. Easwaran, *The Upanishads*, p. 58, Isha Upanishad.

46. Easwaran, *The Upanishads*, p. 59, Isha Upanishad.

47. Easwaran: *The Upanishads*, p. 83, Katha Upanishad.

48. *Jerusalem Bible*, footnote to John 17:3.

49. Easwaran, *The Upanishads*, p. 80, Katha Upanishad.

50. Time Incorporated, *The World's Great Religions* (New York, Time Life, 1957) p. 11.

51. Stephen Hildebrand, *On the Holy Spirit: St. Basil the Great* (Yonkers, NY, St. Vladimir's Seminary Press), p. 55.

52. Hildebrand, *On the Holy Spirit: St. Basil the Great*, p. 89.

53. Hildebrand, *On the Holy Spirit*: *St. Basil the Great*, p. 57.

54. Hildebrand, *On the Holy Spirit*: *St. Basil the Great*, p. 54.

55. Catholic Online (Catholic.org), "Litany of the Blessed Virgin Mary" (August, 2022).

56. Professor K. V. Dev Ed. *The Thousand Names of the Divine Mother* (Sri Lalita Mata Amritanandamayi Center, San Ramon, CA, 1996).

57. Yoga Basics (yogabasics.org), article "Gayatri Mantra," Rig Veda 3. 62. 10.

Bibliography and Brief Review of Sources:

In the order that references to these books appear, here is a bibliography of my primary sources and a brief review of each for those interested in further research.

Jones, Alexander Gen'l Ed., *Jerusalem Bible* (New York: Doubleday & Company 1966)

There are many Bibles available, and the differences in translation, layout, and dogmatic attitude are quite notable. The first difference is that Catholic and Orthodox Bibles, including the Jerusalem, contain all the Wisdom books of the original Septuagint Bible, which contains the Greek Old Testament. The Hebrew and Protestant Bibles, including the King James, do not include the book of Holy Wisdom and Ecclesiasticus which have been copiously quoted in this book and others in the original Septuagint. The Jerusalem Bible also does a nice job of breaking down scripture into line and verse when appropriate to do so, as it is in much of the Wisdom literature of both the Old and New Testaments. There is commentary on each book of the Bible by the editors, which provides for interesting background, and scripture is copiously footnoted and cross-referenced. The *Jerusalem Bible* is a highly recommended, especially those who do not have a Septuagint based Bible. The Old Testament was written in Greek, and the theology and mysticism of the Wisdom books of the Bible are Greek.

Armstrong, Dr. Karen, *The Great Transformation* (Anchor Books 2007)
Armstrong, Dr. Karen, *A History of God* (New York: Glamercy Books, 1993)

Dr. Armstrong is one of the most important Christian theologians and religious book authors of my generation. It is in *A History of God* that I learned that the definition of God as Spirit was "the Energy of God" in the West as well as the East when Jesus was born. We also thank her for the definition of the type of knowledge that God wants us to have of Him/ Her as "the intimate knowledge of God," the same kind Eve had of Adam and the ever-Virgin Mary had of no man. This definition, of course, works well with the mystical Communion of Lover and Beloved in the mystical interpretation of the Song of Songs. Based on what she has written, I expect she could have written this book on Sophia. The problem is, for those following the decisions Constantine dictated in Nicaea, Sophia is not divine or the Holy Spirit. I hear it is a "minor heresy" to believe Sophia is divine. What Christianity has to do instead is be aware that Sophia can save the Church. She is not a threat but an answer to thousands of years of imperial wars and holocausts. Let's once again discover real spirit-based mysticism and work on developing a close personal relationship with our Beloved. But the decision to not allow a Biblical Sophia as the Holy Spirit and grantor of Enlightenment blocks the stream of grace and Spirit emanating from the God Source.

Wiki biographers note Dr. Armstrong is interested in a more mystical Christianity. I don't know anything more mystical than praying to, meditating on, and seeking and finding Sophia the Holy Spirit of Wisdom. Although there is a great gap in class (she is much classer than me), I can't think of a more interesting person to have dinner with. I think she would like my book.

In ***The Great Transformation***, Dr. Armstrong advances the idea that religions were formed as a spiritual reaction against the suffering and horrors of war. Dr. Armstrong stages this transformational change in the distant past, which begs the question of our current spiritual state in a period of continuous wars since 2001. In fact, in many wars, religion is the issue that divides us. Where is the post-transformation peace? Where is the religious transformation our culture went through thousands of years ago? The antidote for wars and holocausts is the realization that we are all members of Christ's Mystical Body such that whatever we do to the least of us, we do to the Christ Consciousness. This is actually true of all sentient beings. We are all connected; we are all one, but human beings are especially sensitive members of God's Mystical Body. The warning is, "Whatever you do to the least of your fellow human beings you do unto Me." The problem with institutions, including several Christian denominations, want to make this an exclusive membership: "I'm part of Christ's mystical body but you aren't because you don't belong to my church." This is the heresy of all religions and ideologies and allows for all the sacrifices and holocausts we have suffered through the ages.

Hixon, Lex, *Great Swan: Meetings with Ramakrishna* (Larson Publications for the Paul Brunton Philosophic Foundation 1992, 1996)

For those not aware of the spiritual revolution that started in India, and now going around the world, this is an important update. Ramakrishna initiated the modern God is Mother movement in India about the time we were fighting the American Indian wars in the United States. It has since spread around the world. Ramakrishna is revered in India even as an Avatar, God in the flesh, and there are many versions of Ramakrishna's life, which was very public. However, many of the India sourced translations of Ramakrishna's life are perhaps to literal in their use of language. Lex Hixon translates Ramakrishna so the subject and meaning flows. We highly recommend this book to all who are interested in Sophia, as She is the Western interpretation of the Mother and the Holy Spirit of the East, Shakti.

Yogananda, *Autobiography of a Yogi* (Los Angeles, CA Self Realization Fellowship 13[th Edition; originally published 1946])

Yogananda, *Autobiography of a Yogi* (New York, Philosophical Library Edition, 1946)

Yes, there are two versions: The "original," published in New York, and the Self Realization Fellowship version, apparently published in the same year. I don't remember the whole story, but it has to do with Yogananda not copywriting the book initially. If the reader is new to Yogananda, buy the Fellowship version as they are a very good organization that is still very active, with beautiful grounds on the Pacific shores of California. I bought the New York version for comparison as this publisher claims the "original," and it does have slightly different content, which I included.

Yogananda's writings are a gift to the Western world. He was an inspired teacher of yogic meditation and practice in the West. He made a huge impression on me back in my college days. He was my first teacher who discussed Christianity in the context of yoga. He brought them together so that Christianity made sense. Yogananda was quite prolific, wrote a number of books, and has a very personable writing style. You can't help but like Yogananda for his sincerity even as he claims minor miracles. The Self Realization Fellowship organization he established has been active ever since and remains a great spiritual resource. They do provide an introductory mail course on meditation, which I recommend as a well-rounded introduction to yogic philosophy and meditation. They also have a strong internet channel with good talks and sermons by a number of Western swamis. They are good people.

Easwaran, Eknath, *The Upanishads* (Lilgiri Press 1987, Blue Mountain Center of Meditation 2007 Tomales, CA)

This is a gem of a book. Easwaran translates the Upanishads based on years of study and his own mystical experience. I am always amazed when reading the Upanishads how much they are like reading the Wisdom books of the Bible with all the "buried treasure" with "kingdoms" and "cities of God." And again, like the Wisdom books of the Bible, the Upanishads are religious love poetry broken down by line and verse. Not only is the translation great but his introductions to the book and the individual Upanishads are enlightening.

Harvard Classics, Volume: *Plato, Epictetus, Marcus Aurelius, (and Cleanthes)* (New York, P. F. Collier and Son 1909, 1937)
Volume: *Bacon, Milton, Brown*

I picked up the entire set of Harvard Classics all stacked in a box for about ten bucks at a used book sale at the library. What's neat about this set is that these are classic translations of ancient poetry and proverbs from a time when these writings were considered to be more important than they are now. Comparing Harvard's translation of Cleanthes' Hymn to those of more recent times, reveals a certain bias against Greek concepts that are important in modern Christianity. I use this collection as a historical encyclopedia of classic Western thought.

Stanley, Thomas, *Pythagoras: His Life and Teachings, A Compendium of Classical Sources* (Lake Worth, Fl, Ibis Press, 2010)

The main text of this book, the mainstay of Pythagoras research, "was written by Thomas Stanley and first published in 1687 in The History of Philosophy." It is perhaps surprising that a book written in 1687 would be the most quoted work on Pythagoras. I don't know if this is because the sources Stanley worked with are now missing, or there is not as much interest in Pythagoras now as there was then. However, Pythagoras, the first lover of Sophia, the first philosopher, was an incredibly important spiritual teacher and theologian, "The Buddha of the West," who connects the Western philosophy to the East and mystical yoga.

Schiff, Stacy, *Cleopatra, a Life,* (Little Brown and Company, 2010)

This book contains a detailed description of the corruption, excesses, wars, genocides, and fratricides of the Ptolemaic Dynasty. The Ptolemaic Dynasty, of which Cleopatra was a member as was her husband, earlier commissioned the Pentateuch, including the law books of the Bible. This book provides a great description of what the times were like in Alexandria, Egypt, when the Bible was written and published there about 30 years before Jesus was born. Stacy's writing style is flawless, and as she already won a Pulitzer Prize, what more can I add? This is a very interesting, well-written book.

Keay, John, *India, A History* (New York, Grove Press/ Grove Atlantic 2000, 2010)

Hail Sophia makes the point that India is the source of much of our philosophical, spiritual, religious, and mystical traditions even here in the West, even in the Judeo-Christian tradition. In India they have a different concept of how the Western, Judeo-Christian tradition developed than most Westerners.

Funk, Robert W., Hoover, Roy W., and the Jesus Seminar, *The Five Gospels: The Search for the Authentic Words of Jesus* (Harper SanFransisco,1993)

The Jesus Seminar uses the Gospel of Thomas, the fifth Gospel, for scholarly analysis of the New Testament traditions and its history.

Meyer, Marvin and Bloom, Harold, *The Gospel of St. Thomas: The Hidden Sayings of Jesus* (New York, HarperCollins Publishers, 1992)

This is a more complicated version of Jesus' parables but still the same parables. This Gospel is so well covered that it is broken down by verse. There are numerous versions of the Gospel and of its interpretation.

Harvey, Andrew *Teachings of Christian Mystics* (Boston, Shambhala Pocket Library, 1997)

Andrew is a highly regarded and prolific writer on the subject of both Eastern and Western Mysticism. This is an enjoyable anthology of insights from Western mystics.

Ed. Times Books Ltd, *The Times Atlas of World History* (London: Times Books Limited, (1984)

A large coffee table book I found to be useful in understanding the history of the times in which the Wisdom books were written. I found it in a used bookstore. It is perhaps indicative of the sentiment of these British historians that they would name one chapter "The Americas on the Eve of European Conquest." Few but the most diehard imperialists would admit such a thing. The book is filled with arrows of one kingdom and peoples invading another. That's how we got to be here.

Finkelstein, Israel and Silberman, Neil Asher, *The Bible Unearthed*, (Touchstone Book/ Simon and Shuster worldwide, 2001)

So these present day Jewish scholars don't think the Pentateuch is historically accurate, joining the critics of Christianity who think it is all made up. Well, maybe that's the point. In this book, present day Jewish scholars demonstrate they don't believe the Pentateuch is historically accurate, joining the critics of Christianity who point to the same documents to prove Christianity is a bad religion. They forget entirely that Jesus and the Prophets opposed many of the laws and imperial social attitudes. Jesus elevated the human being as connected to His own Mystical Body such that whatever we do to the least of our brothers, we do to Jesus Christ.

Hildebrand, Stephen, *On the Holy Spirit: Basil the Great,* (Yonkers, NY St. Popular Patristics Series, Vladimir's Seminary Press 2011)

This is a well-written, concise (about 120 pages) account of St. Basil the Great's work on the Holy Spirit, which makes it a great resource. Basil didn't quite get us back to the personality and attractiveness of Sophia, but he saved the Holy Spirit as the giver of Life and Enlightenment. Basil experienced God as Holy Spirit, and the Roman male version remains in the Creed. From there, it is easy to get back to Sophia.

Professor K. V. Dev Ed., *The Thousand Names of the Divine Mother, Sri Lalita Sahasranama* (Mata Amritanandamayi Center, San Ramon, CA, 1996)

Like the Self Realization Fellowship, this is a very good organization and recommended resource for worship of the Mother in the Hindu devotional tradition. Ma, or the Hugging Saint, has a wide following in both India and the US.

Internet Resource Sites:

Wikipedia

Although Wikipedia tries to be an authoritative internet encyclopedia for all, I was told by an advisor to never trust Wikipedia or use it as a reference in footnotes. I don't know if this is part of the information vs. disinformation controversy, and who do you believe nowadays(?), but I can tell you that on the history of Israel, or Israel and Judea, or Israel and Judah, there are versions to satisfy anyone in the political spectrum, including ours. Which to trust? I don't trust Wikipedia on controversial topics but for dates and names of battles why not. I used Wikipedia on Ptolemy VIII because it fit the story, and I think it is accurate.

Yoga Basics (yogabasics.org)

This is a good resource on yoga philosophy.

Catholic Online (Catholic.org)

An authoritative Catholic resource site.

Articles on Ancient History (Livius.org)

So while researching Alexander the Great I found this scholarly site which seemed to summarize why people considered the conquests of Alexander to be so great. Their observations were on Plutarch's arguments on behalf of Alexander. I don't think this is their opinion but a scholarly observation.

Communicating With Sophia:

If you would like to communicate with Sophia directly – ask Her questions, offer a prayer or intention, confess an error, make an appeal, express your gratitude, or even give a cry of oppression and disappointment – whatever you write on these pages Sophia will hear immediately and answer, providing answers, council, comfort, and grace.

Reader's Notes:

Reader's Notes:

Reader's Notes:

Author Biography:

Jim McGilbrith is an independently minded, over-educated, professor of his love for Sophia at the Jim McG Forest School of Philosophy. Out in the forests of rural Wisconsin, Jim spends time chopping wood, carrying water, feeding the birds, watching sunrises, making woodcraft and art, cutting down trees, burning firewood on wintery nights, haunting used bookstores, meditating on Sophia, and writing on the subject of his Eternal Beloved in his cabin in the woods with his spouse, herself a reflection of Sophia. His human beloved doesn't understand how special she is, which makes Jim smile in appreciation and wonder at Sophia and the Wisdom of Her creation.

Made in the USA
Monee, IL
03 March 2023